BEATLES forever

T0045636

ISBN 978-0-634-02575-4

HAL•LEONARD®
CORPORATION
7777 W. BLUEMOUND RD. P.O. BOX 13819 MILWAUKEE, WI 53213

Visit Hal Leonard Online at
www.halleonard.com

contents

ALL MY LOVING

Words and Music by JOHN LENNON
and PAUL McCARTNEY

Bright rock and roll

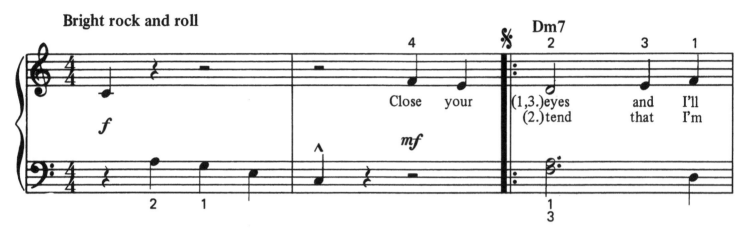

Close your (1,3.)eyes and I'll
(2.)tend that I'm

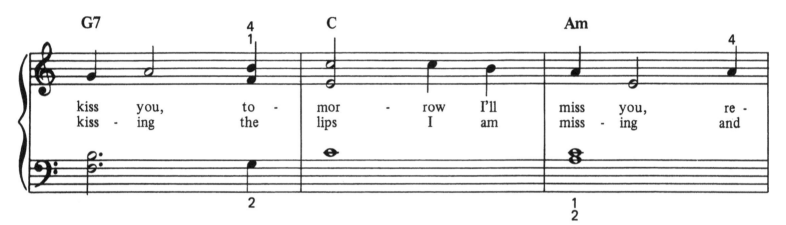

kiss you, to - mor - row I'll miss you, re -
kiss - ing to the lips I am miss - ing and

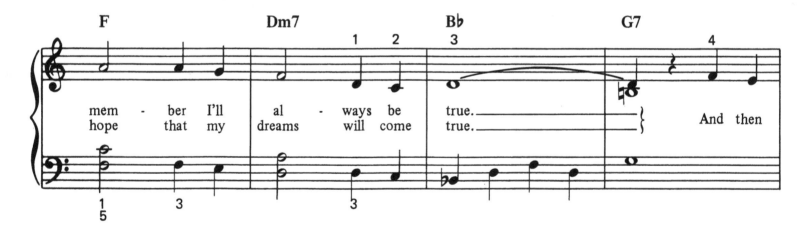

mem - ber I'll al - ways be true.
hope that my dreams will come true. And then

while I'm a - way, I'll write home ev - 'ry day, ___ and I'll

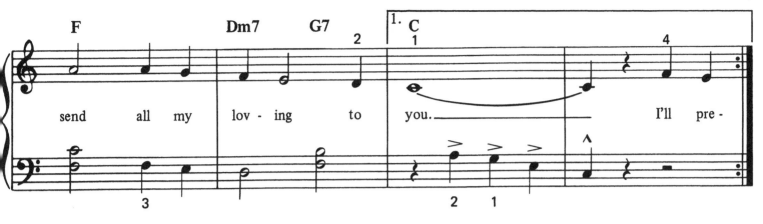

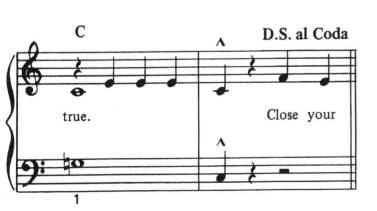

AND I LOVE HER

Words and Music by JOHN LENNON
and PAUL McCARTNEY

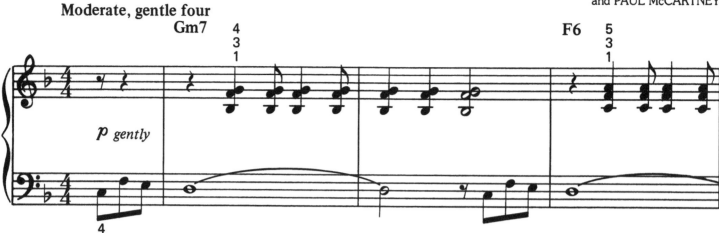

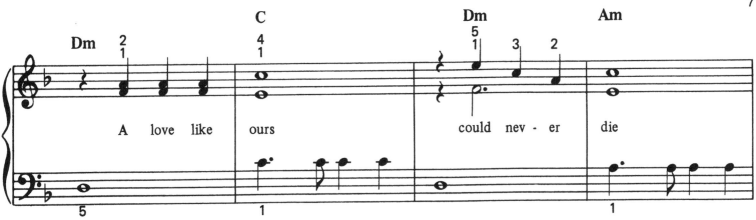

A love like ours could nev - er die

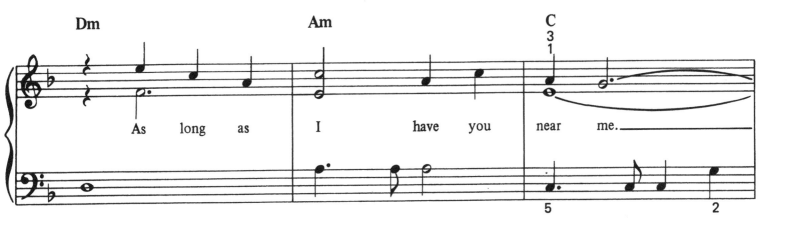

As long as I have you near me.____

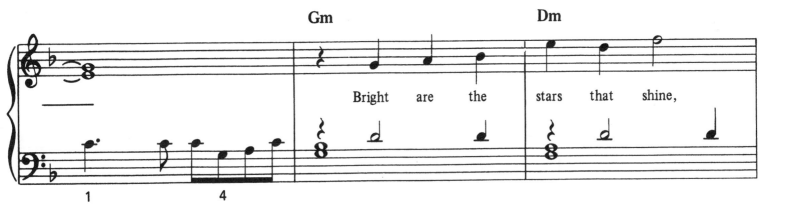

____ Bright are the stars that shine,

dark is the sky;____ I know this

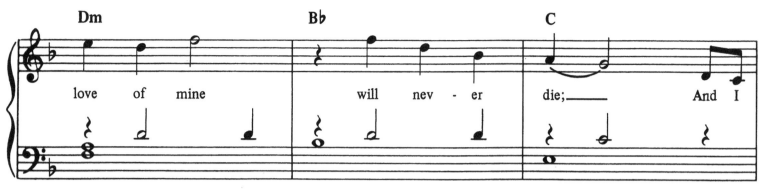

love of mine will nev - er die;_____ And I

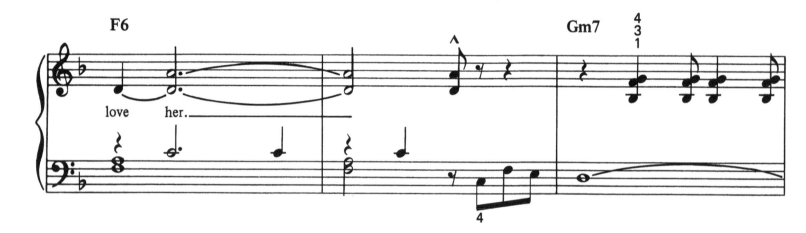

love her.

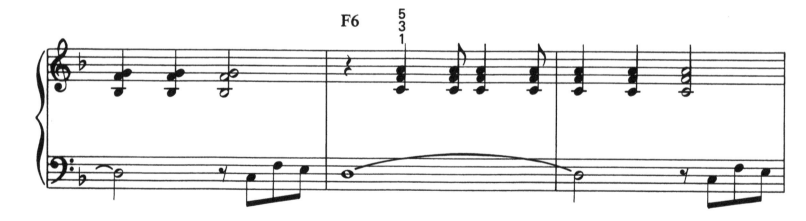

slowing

BECAUSE

Words and Music by JOHN LENNON
and PAUL McCARTNEY

Moderately Slow

ped. sim.

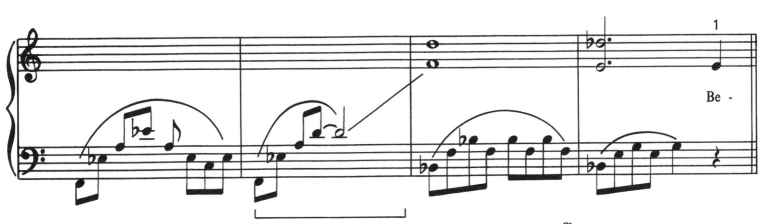

Be -

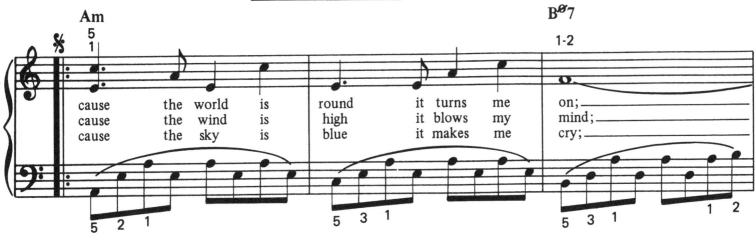

cause the world is round it turns me on;
cause the wind is high it blows my mind;
cause the sky is blue it makes me cry;

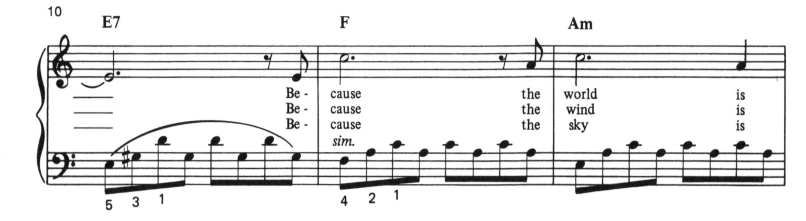

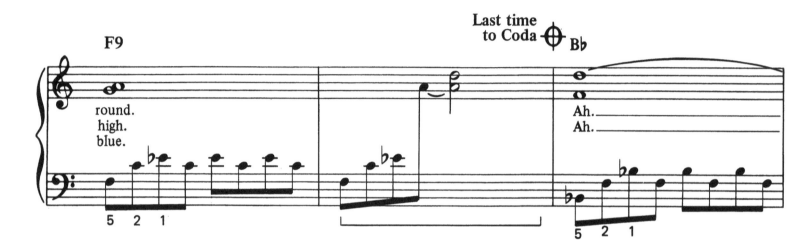

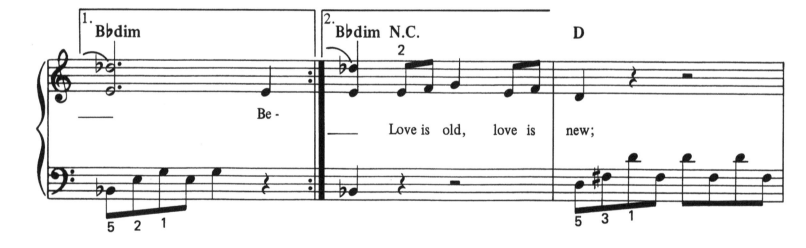

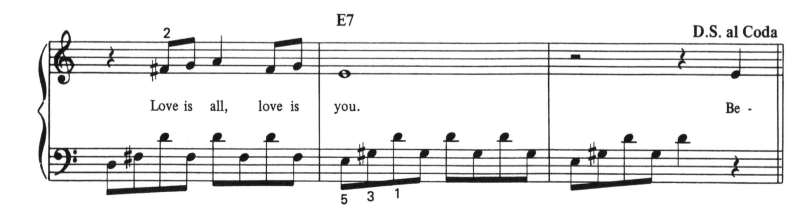

A DAY IN THE LIFE

Words and Music by JOHN LENNON
and PAUL McCARTNEY

Slow 4

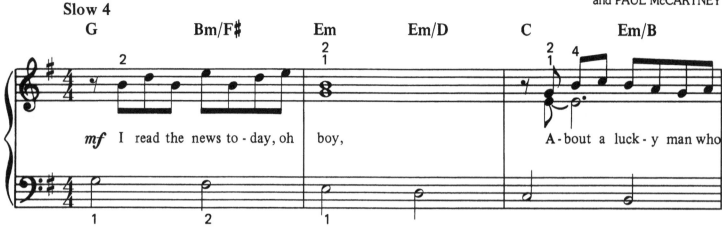

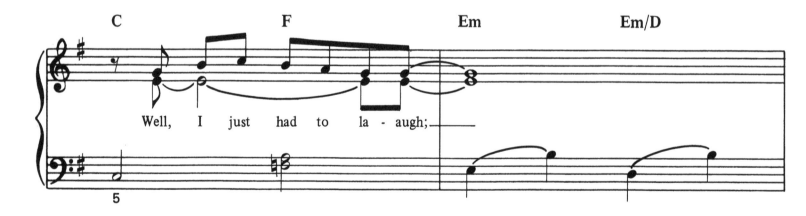

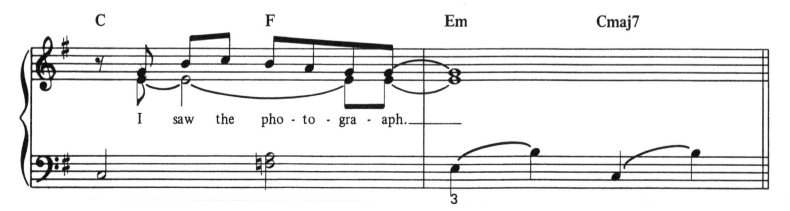

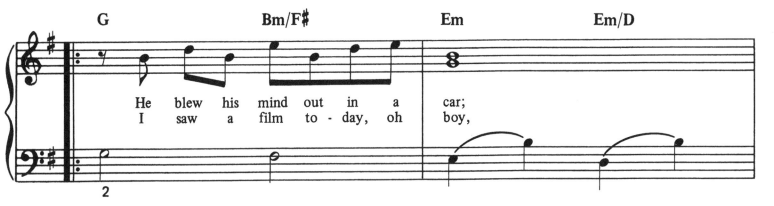

He blew his mind out in a car;
I saw a film to - day, oh boy,

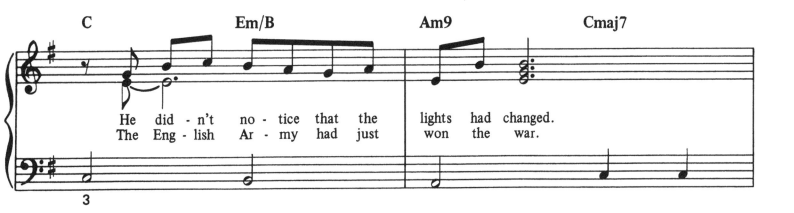

He did - n't no - tice that the lights had changed.
The Eng - lish Ar - my had just won the war.

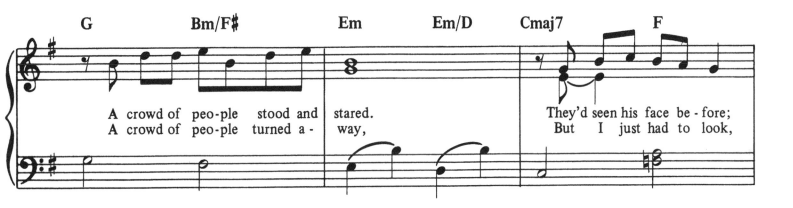

A crowd of peo - ple stood and stared.
A crowd of peo - ple turned a - way,

They'd seen his face be - fore;
But I just had to look,

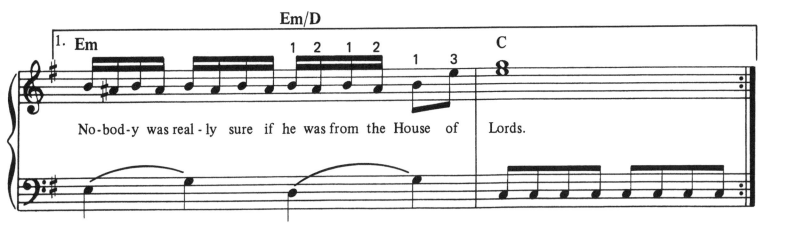

No - bod - y was real - ly sure if he was from the House of Lords.

Hav-ing read the book, I'd love to turn

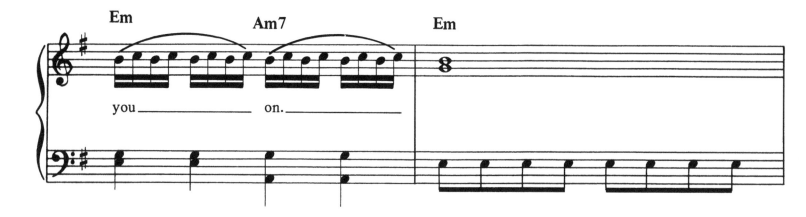

you _____ on. _____

Twice as fast (♪ = ♩)

Woke up, got out of bed; Dragged a comb a-cross my

head. Found my way down stairs and

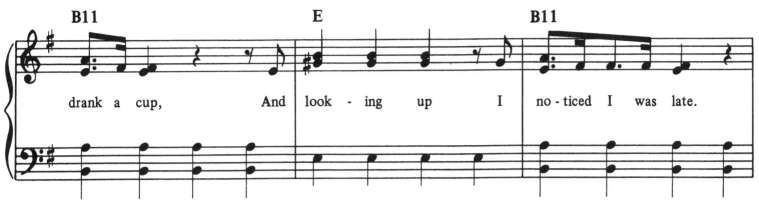

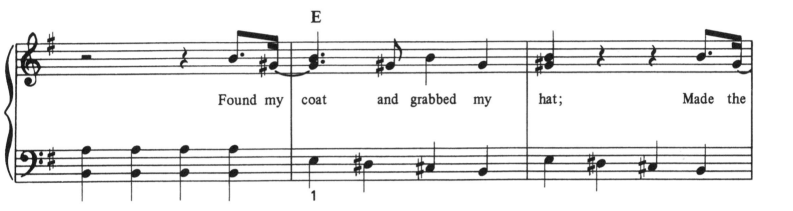

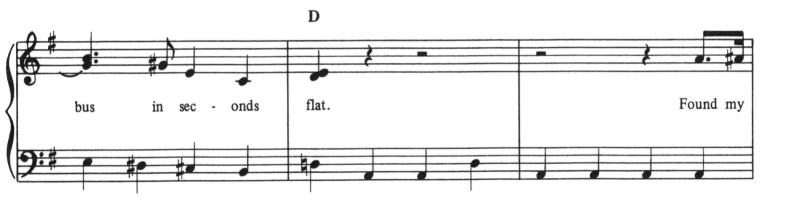

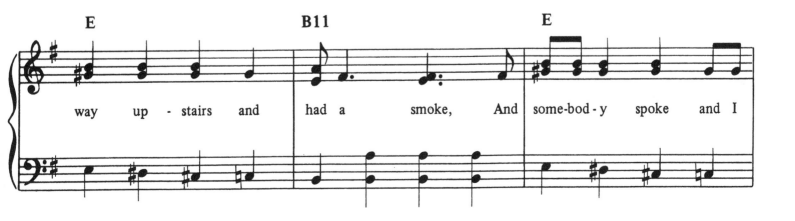

Original tempo

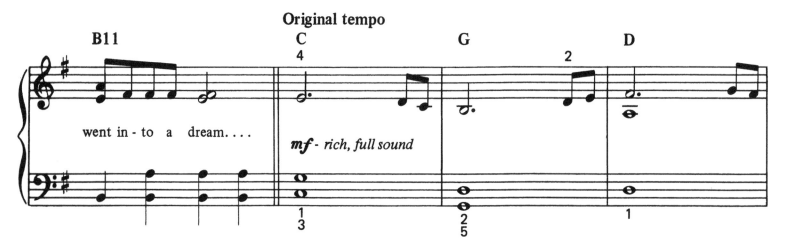

went in-to a dream....

mf - rich, full sound

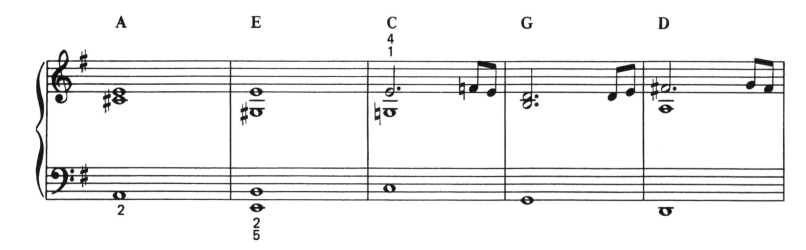

I read the news to-day, oh

boy,

Four thou-sand holes in Black-burn,

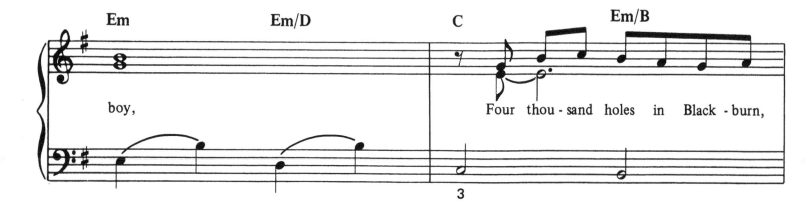

Lan-ca-shire. And though the holes were ra-ther small,

They had to count them all. Now they know how man-y holes it takes to fill the Al-bert

Hall; I'd love to turn _____ you _____

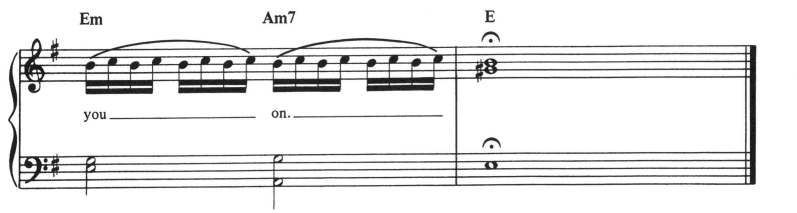

you _____ on. _____

DRIVE MY CAR

Words and Music by JOHN LENNON
and PAUL McCARTNEY

With a beat

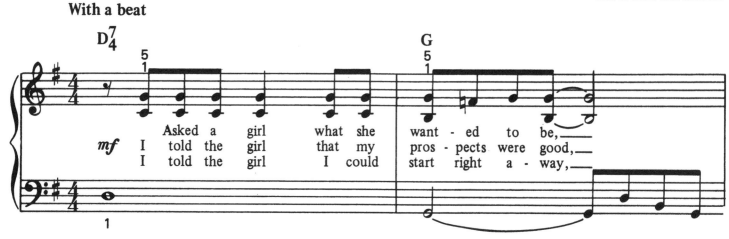

Asked a girl what she want-ed to be,___
I told the girl that my pros-pects were good,___
I told the girl I could start right a-way,___

She said, "Ba-by, can't you see?___
And she said, "Ba-by, it's un-der-stood.___
And she said, "Listen, babe, I got some-thing to say.___

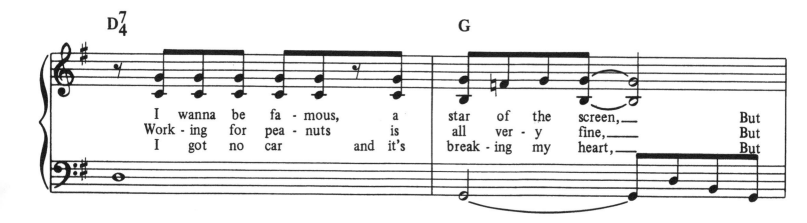

I wan-na be fa-mous, a star of the screen,___ But
Work-ing for pea-nuts is all ver-y fine,___ But
I got no car and it's break-ing my heart,___ But

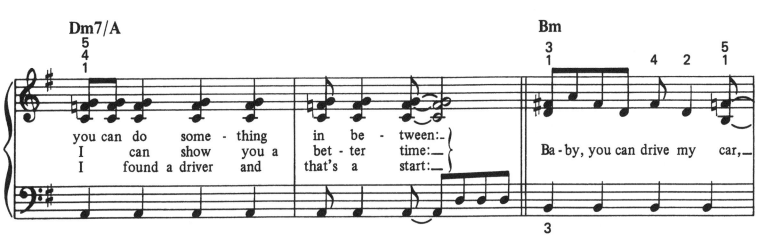

you can do some-thing / in be-tween:
I can show you a / bet-ter time:
I found a driver and / that's a start:

Ba-by, you can drive my car,

Yes, I'm gon-na be a star,

Ba-by, you can drive my car and may-be I'll love you."

Beep beep mm beep beep, yeah!

FROM ME TO YOU

Words and Music by JOHN LENNON
and PAUL McCARTNEY

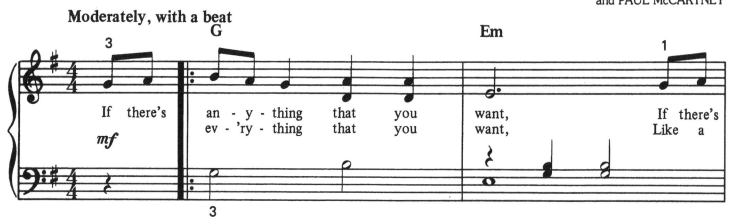

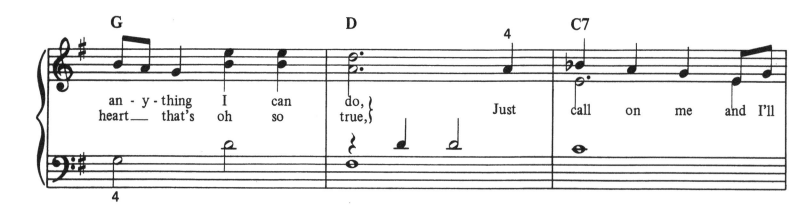

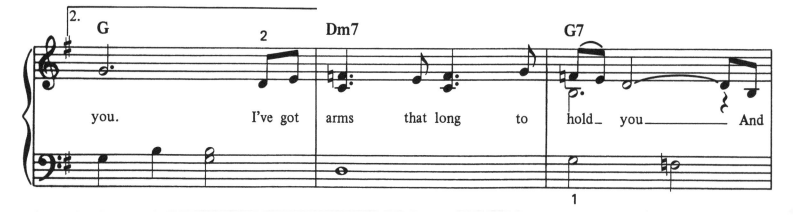

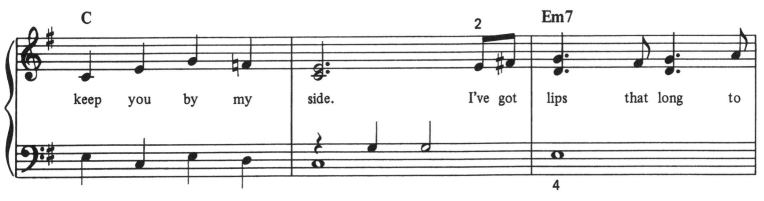

keep you by my side. I've got lips that long to

kiss__ you And keep you sat - is - fied. If there's

an - y - thing that you want, If there's an - y - thing I can do, Just

call on me and I'll send it a - long__ with love from me__ to you.__

GETTING BETTER

Words and Music by JOHN LENNON
and PAUL McCARTNEY

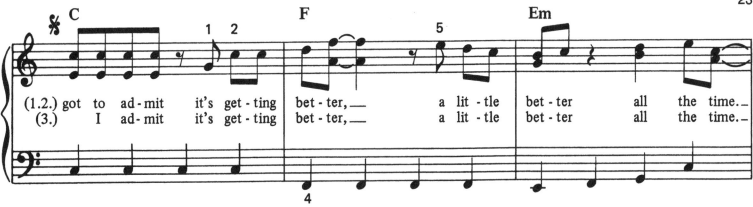

C   F   Em

(1.2.) got to ad-mit it's get-ting bet-ter, ___ a lit-tle bet-ter all the time. ___
(3.) I ad-mit it's get-ting bet-ter, ___ a lit-tle bet-ter all the time. ___

Dm7   G   C   F

I have to ad-mit it's get-ting bet-ter, ___
yes I ad-mit it's get-ting bet-ter, ___ it's get-ting

Em   Dm7   1. G7

bet-ter ___ since you've been mine. ___

2. Me

2.3. F C F C   F C F N.C.   C

Get - ting so much bet - ter all the time. It's get-ting bet-ter all the

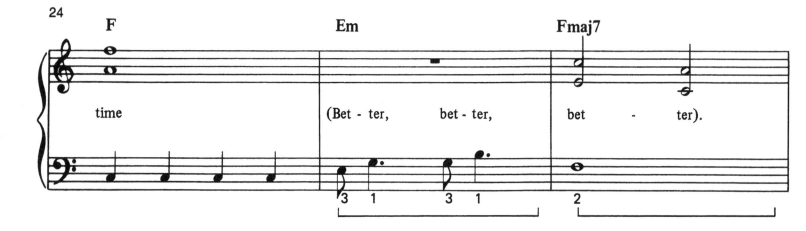

F

time

Em

(Bet - ter, bet - ter,

Fmaj7

bet - ter).

C

It's get - ting bet - ter all the

F

time

Em

(Bet - ter, bet - ter,

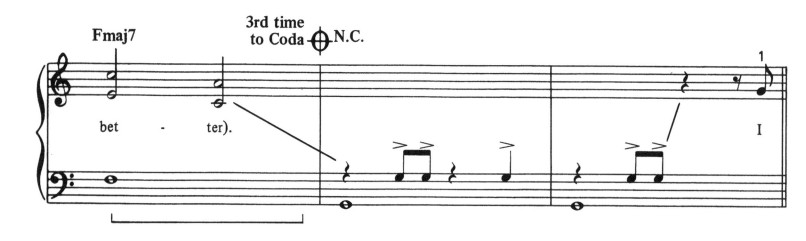

Fmaj7

bet - ter).

3rd time to Coda ⊕ **N.C.**

1

I

G7

used to be cruel ___ to my wom - an, I beat ___ her and kept ___

her a - part__ from the things__ that she loved.__

Man, I was mean,__ but I'm chang - ing my scene,__ and I'm do -

D.S. al Coda
(take 3rd lyric
and 3rd ending)

- ing the best__ that I can.__

CODA

F	C	F	C	F	C	F	C

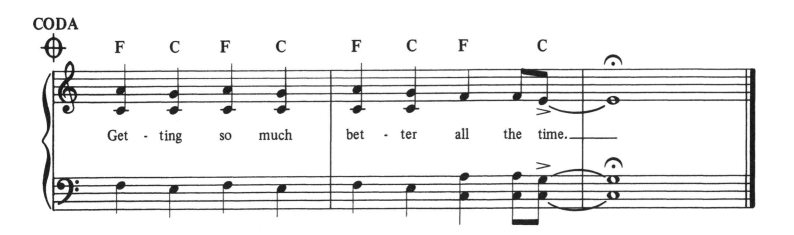

Get - ting so much bet - ter all the time.__

GOT TO GET YOU INTO MY LIFE

Words and Music by JOHN LENNON
and PAUL McCARTNEY

Very steady, with a lilt

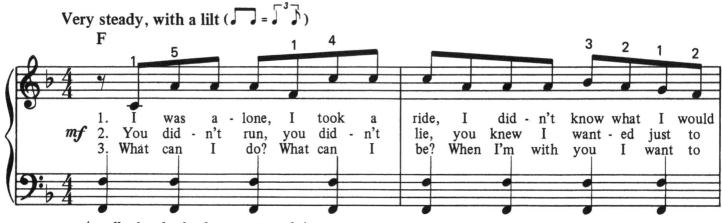

1. I was a - lone, I took a ride, I did - n't know what I would
2. You did - n't run, you did - n't lie, you knew I want - ed just to
3. What can I do? What can I be? When I'm with you I want to

(smaller hands play lower notes only)

find there.
hold you.
stay there.

An - oth - er road where may - be
And had you gone, you knew in
If I'm true I'll nev - er

I could see an - oth - er kind of mind there.
time we'd meet a - gain for I'd have told you.
leave, and if I do I know the way there.

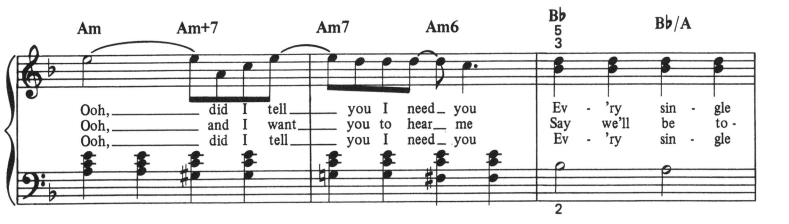

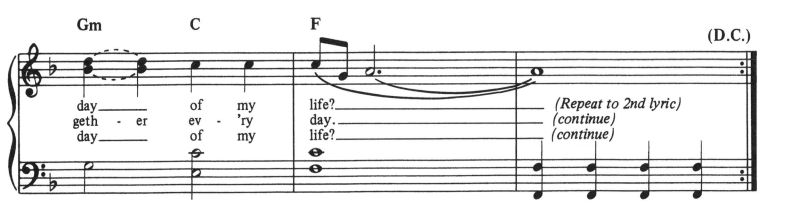

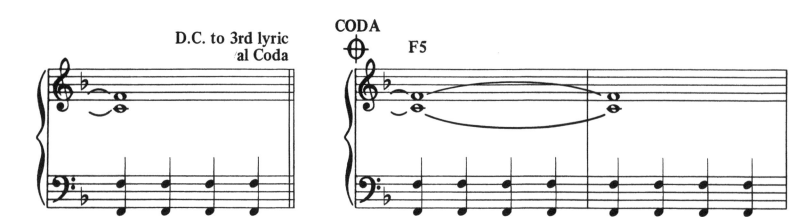

Got to get you in - to my life!

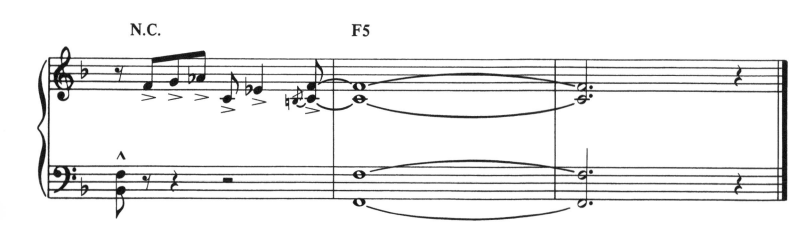

HERE COMES THE SUN

Words and Music by
GEORGE HARRISON

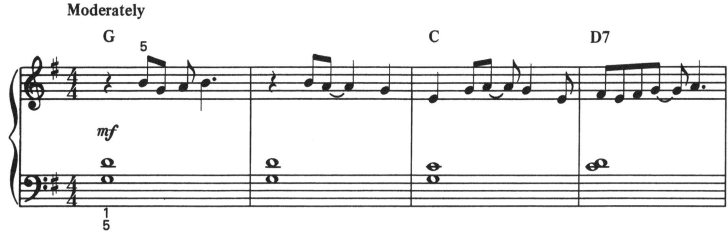

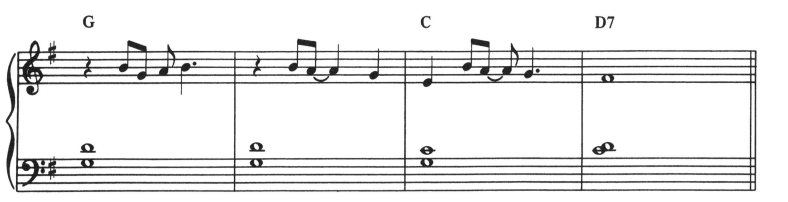

Here comes_ the sun, doo da doo doo. Here comes_ the

sun, And I say, "It's all right."

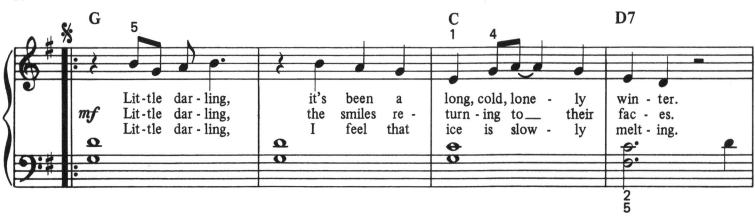

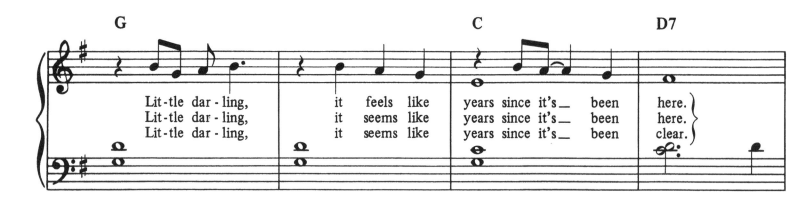

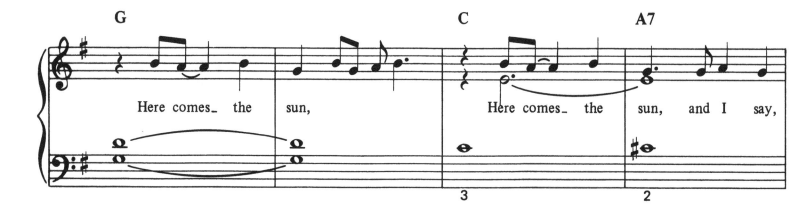

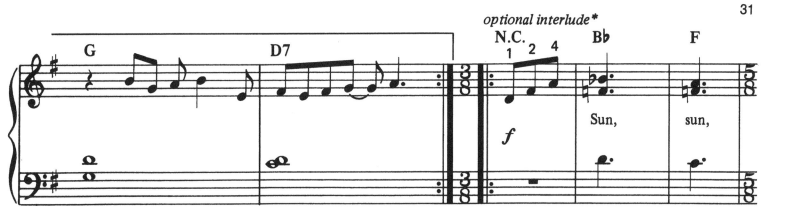

optional interlude

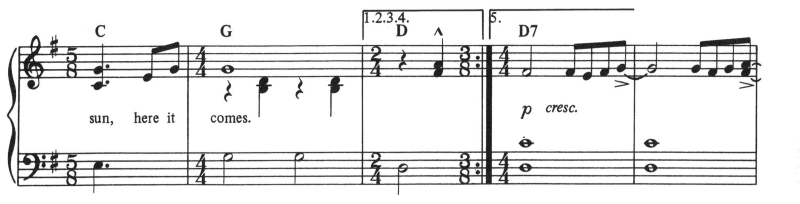

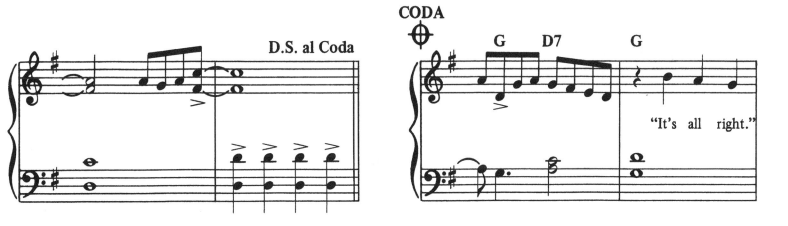

D.S. al Coda

CODA

*If omitted, go directly to Coda

HEY JUDE

Words and Music by JOHN LENNON
and PAUL McCARTNEY

Slow and steady

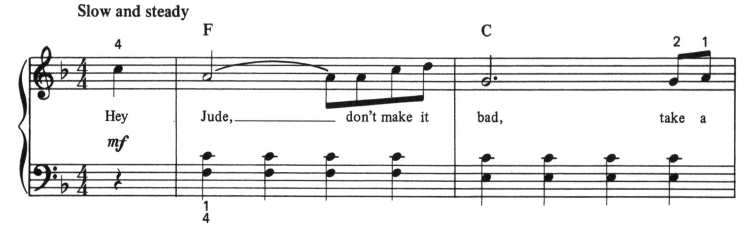

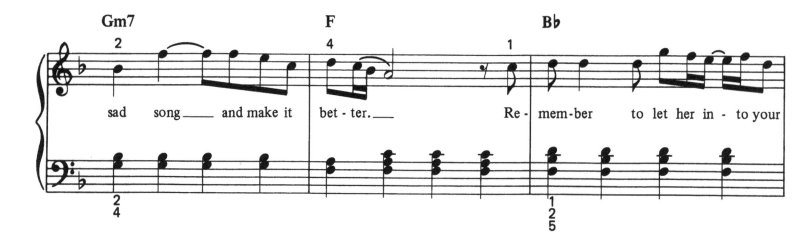

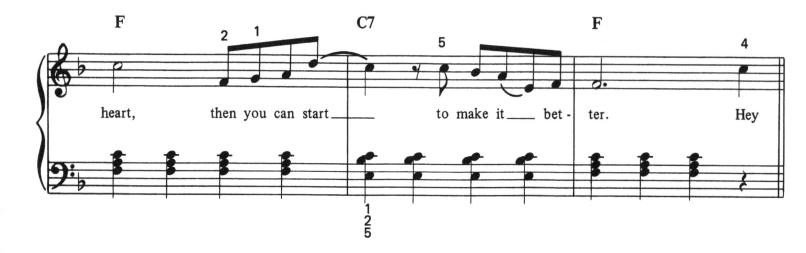

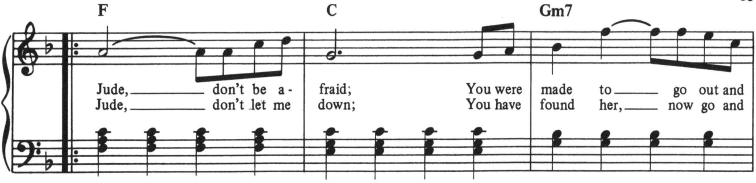

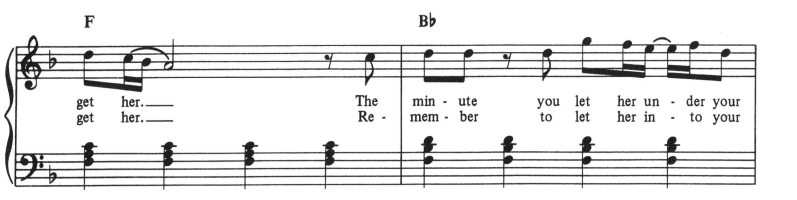

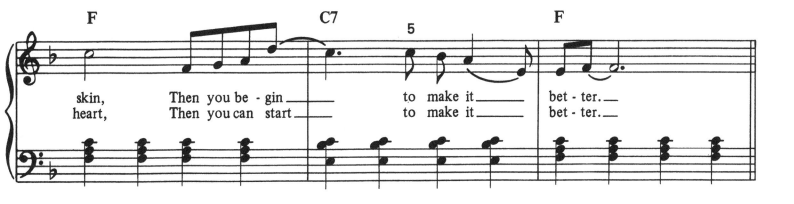

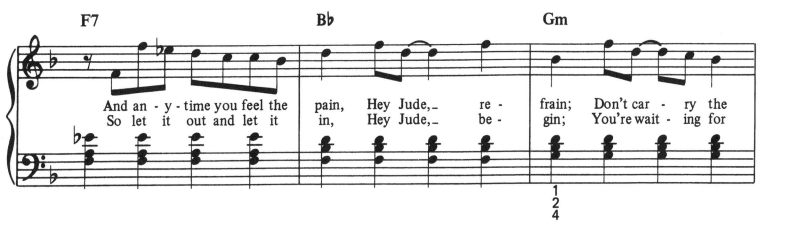

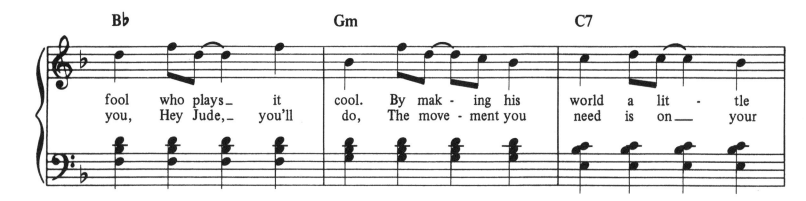

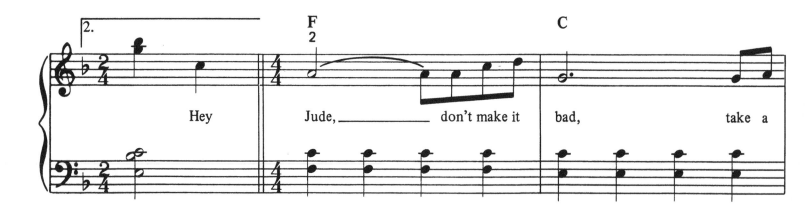

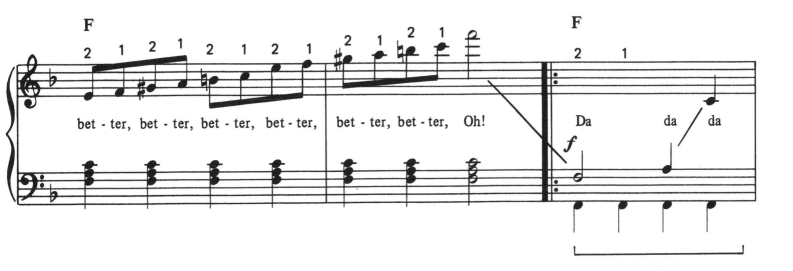

I SAW HER STANDING THERE

Words and Music by JOHN LENNON
and PAUL McCARTNEY

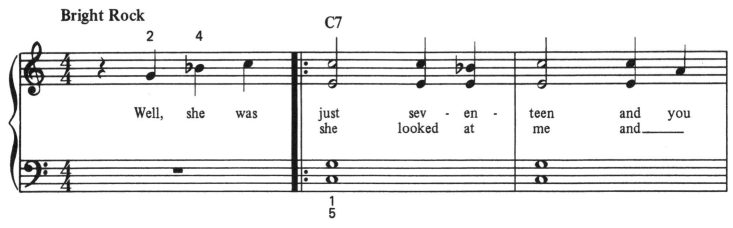

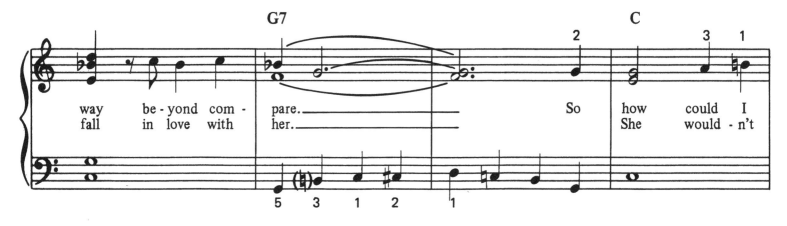

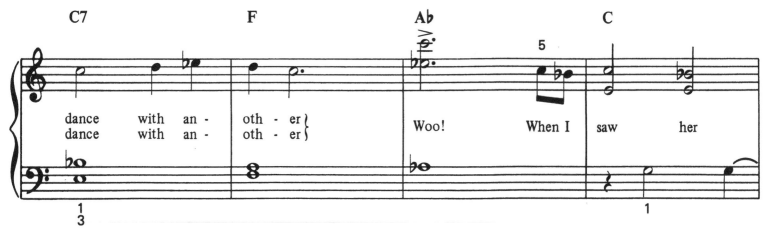

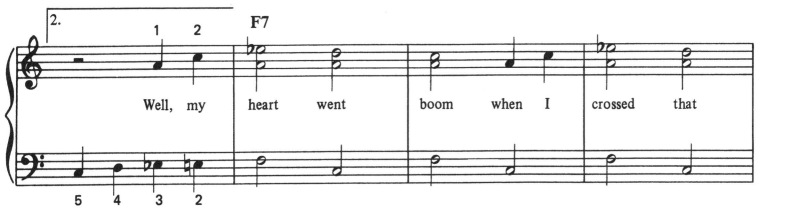

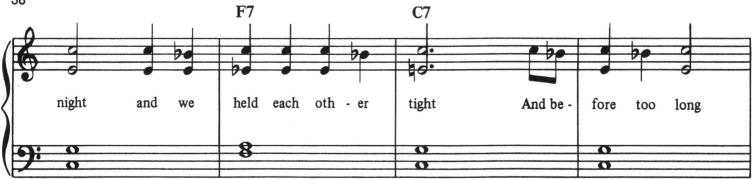

night and we held each oth - er tight And be - fore too long

I fell in love with her. Now I'll nev - er

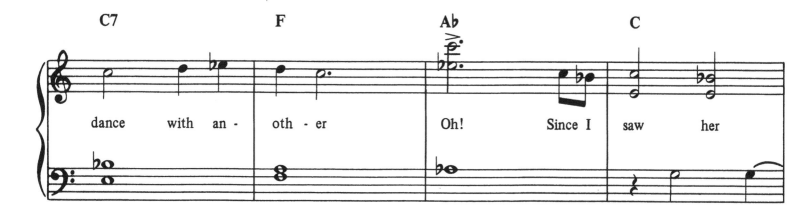

dance with an - oth - er Oh! Since I saw her

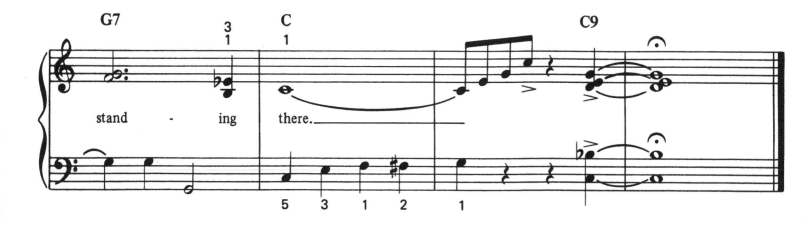

stand - ing there.

I'M LOOKING THROUGH YOU

Words and Music by JOHN LENNON
and PAUL McCARTNEY

Moderately, with a beat

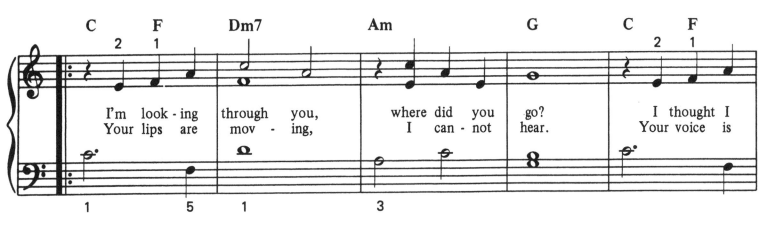

I'm look-ing through you,
Your lips are mov - ing,

where did you go?
I can-not hear.

I thought I
Your voice is

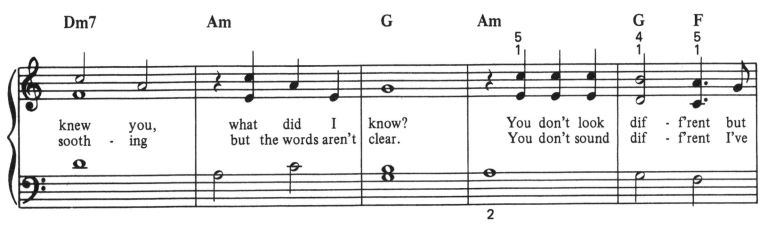

knew you,
sooth - ing

what did I
but the words aren't

know?
clear.

You don't look
You don't sound

dif - f'rent but
dif - f'rent I've

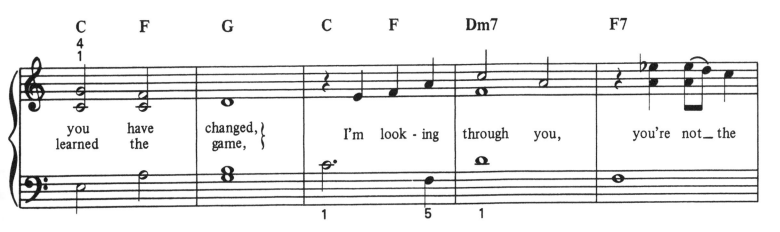

you have the
learned the

changed,
game,

I'm look - ing

through you,

you're not the

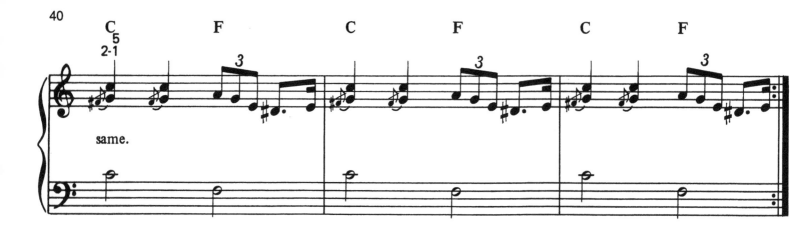

same.

Why, tell me why, did you not treat me right?___

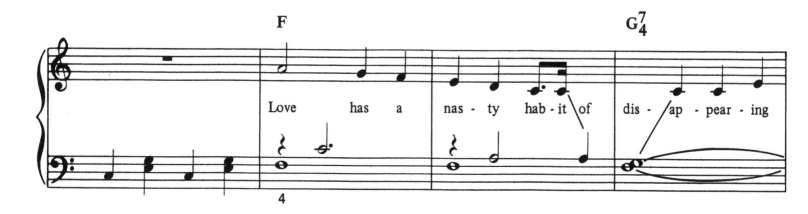

Love has a nas-ty hab-it of dis-ap-pear-ing

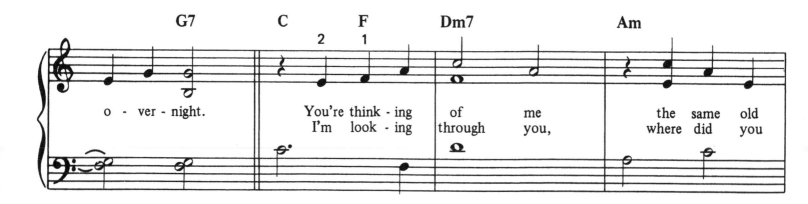

o - ver-night.

You're think-ing of me the same old
I'm look-ing through you, where did you

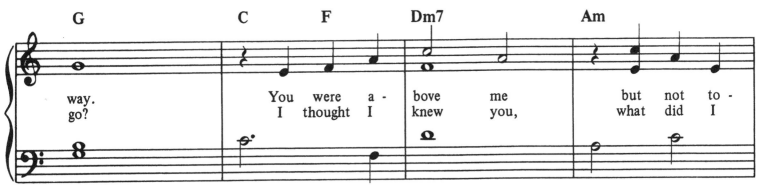

G   C   F   Dm7   Am

way.
go?   You were a - bove me   but not to -
         I thought I knew you,   what did I

G   Am   G   F   C   F

day.
know?   The on - ly dif - f'rence is you're down
         You don't look dif - f'rent, but you have

2

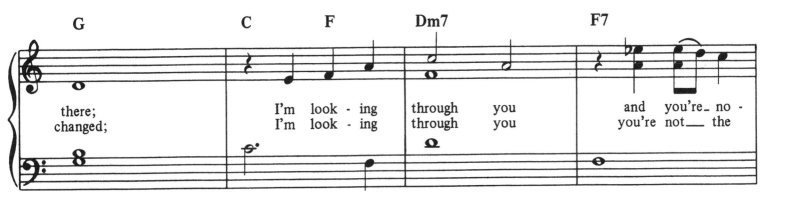

G   C   F   Dm7   F7

there;
changed;   I'm look - ing through you   and you're_ no -
         I'm look - ing through you   you're not_ the

**After repeat,
fade on last 4 measures**

C   F   C   F   C   F   C   F

where!
same.

I WANNA BE YOUR MAN

Words and Music by JOHN LENNON
and PAUL McCARTNEY

Medium Rock

1.3. I wan-na be your lov - er, ba - by, I wan-na be your man;
2. Tell me___ that you love me, ba - by, let me___ un - der - stand;

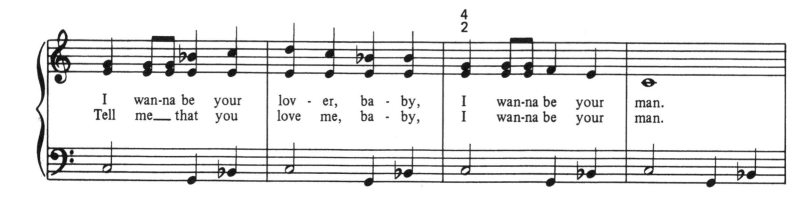

I wan-na be your lov - er, ba - by, I wan-na be your man.
Tell me___ that you love me, ba - by, I wan-na be your man.

Love you like no oth - er, ba - by, like no oth - er can;
I wan-na be your lov - er, ba - by, I wan-na be your man;

Love you like no oth - er, ba - by, like no oth - er can.
I wan-na be your lov - er, ba - by, I wan-na be your man;

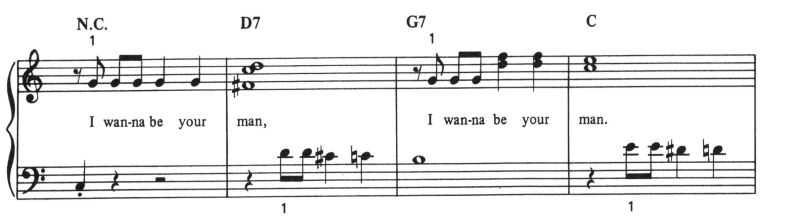

N.C.　　　D7　　　G7　　　C

I wan-na be your man, I wan-na be your man.

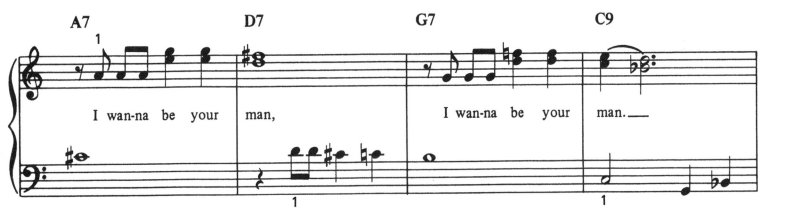

A7　　　D7　　　G7　　　C9

I wan-na be your man, I wan-na be your man.____

play 3 times　C7　　　C　Gm7　　C　Repeat and Fade

I wan-na be your man,____

I'VE JUST SEEN A FACE

Words and Music by JOHN LENNON
and PAUL McCARTNEY

I've just seen a face; I can't for - get the time_ or place where we just

met. She's just the girl for me, and I want all_ the world to see we've

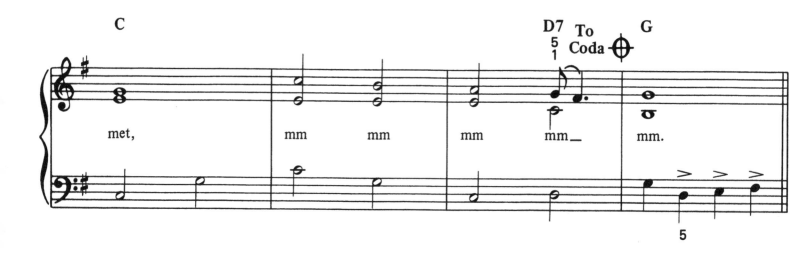

met, mm mm mm mm_ mm.

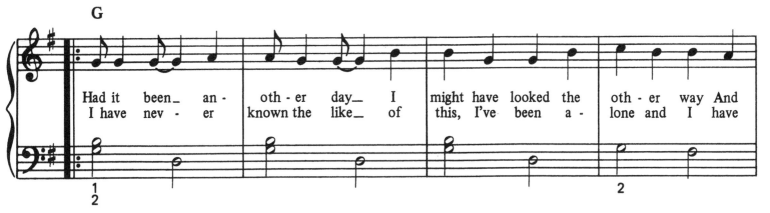

G

Had it been_ an- | oth - er day_ I | might have looked the | oth - er way And
I have nev - er | known the like_ of | this, I've been a - | lone and I have

Em

I'd have nev - er | been a - ware_ But | as it is I'll | dream of her to-
missed things and_ kept | out of sight,_ For | oth - er girls were | nev - er quite like

C   **D7**   **G**

night, }
this, }
     da   da   da   da da   da.

D   **C**

Fall - ing,_ | yes I am fall - ing,_ | And she keeps

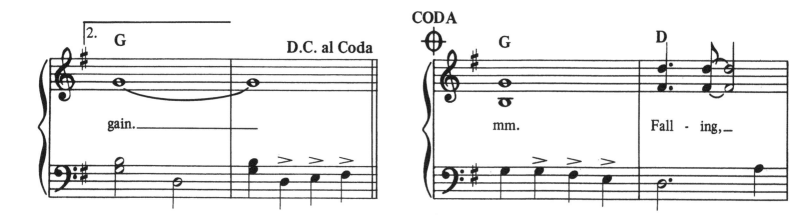

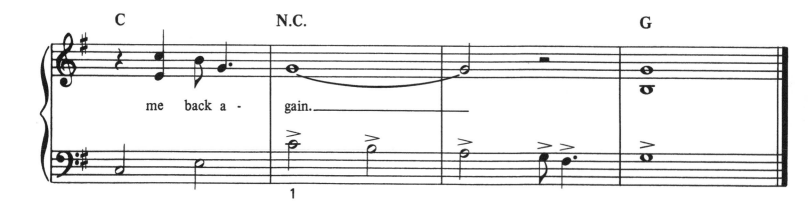

IT WON'T BE LONG

Words and Music by JOHN LENNON
and PAUL McCARTNEY

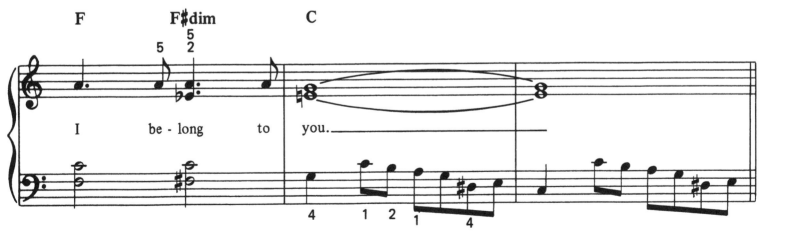

48

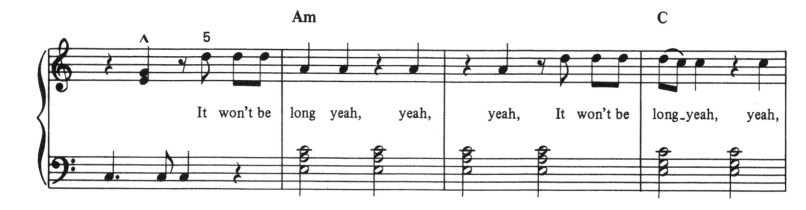

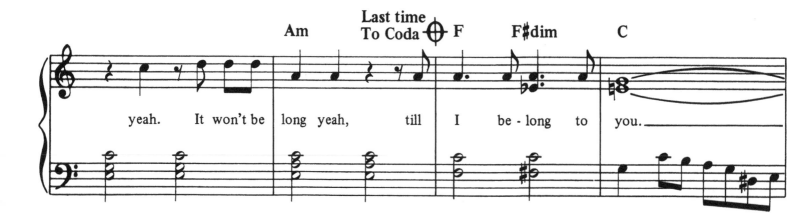

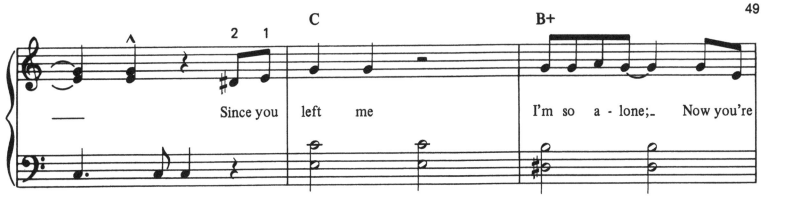

Since you left me I'm so a-lone;__ Now you're

com-ing, you're com-ing on home.__ I'll be good like I

know I should, you're com-ing home!__ you're com-ing home!__

home!__ So

I be-long to__ you.

IN MY LIFE

Words and Music by JOHN LENNON
and PAUL McCARTNEY

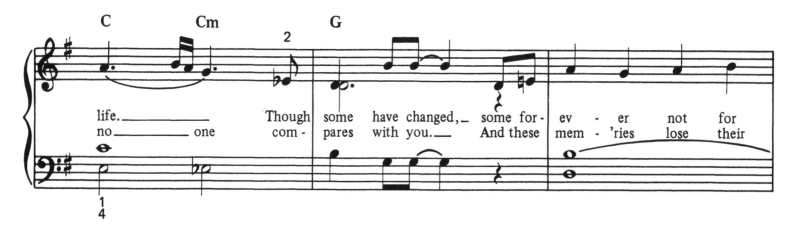

51

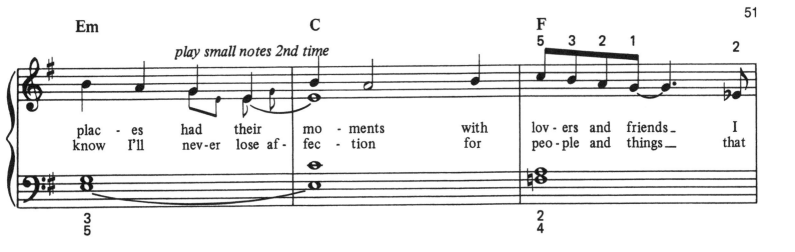

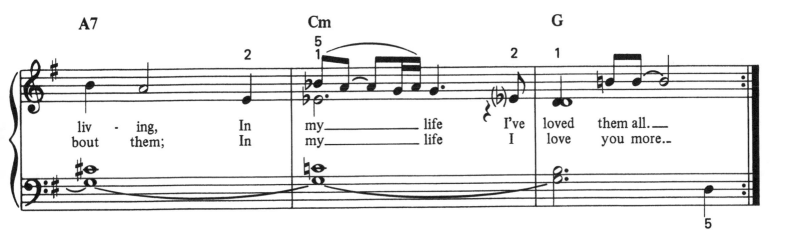

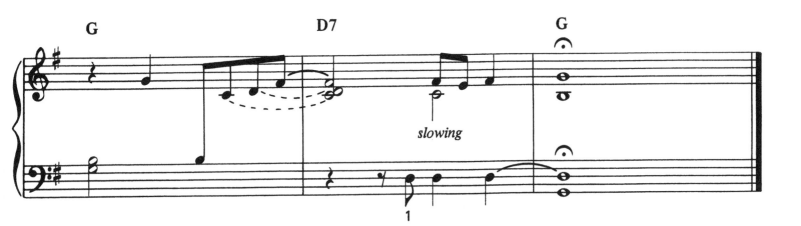

IT'S ONLY LOVE

Words and Music by JOHN LENNON
and PAUL McCARTNEY

Moderately

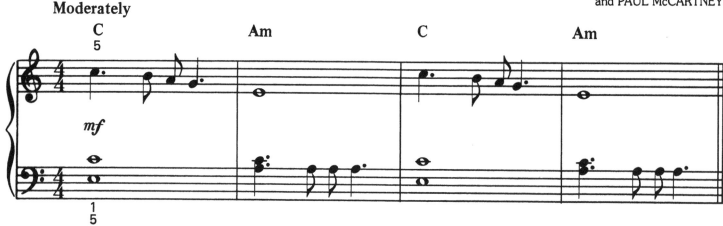

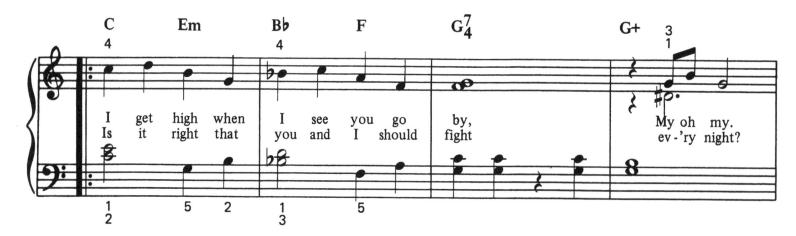

I get high when   I see you go   by,   My oh my.
Is it right when that   you and I should   fight   ev -'ry night?

When you sigh, my,   my in - side just   flies,   but - ter - flies.
Just the sight of   you makes night - time   bright,   ver - y bright.

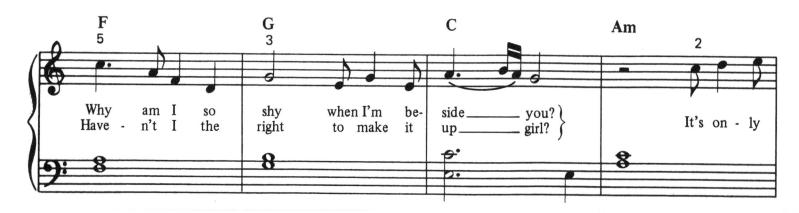

Why am I so   shy when I'm be -   side ___ you?   It's on - ly
Have - n't I the   right to make it   up ___ girl?

love, and that is all, Why should I feel the way I do? It's on - ly

love, and that is all, But it's so hard lov-ing you.

you, Yes, it's so hard___ lov-ing you, lov-ing you.

slowing

MARTHA MY DEAR

Words and Music by JOHN LENNON
and PAUL McCARTNEY

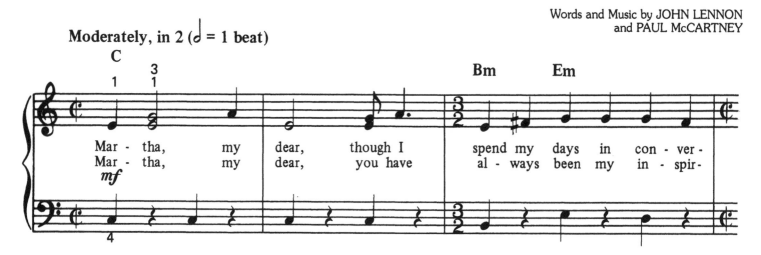

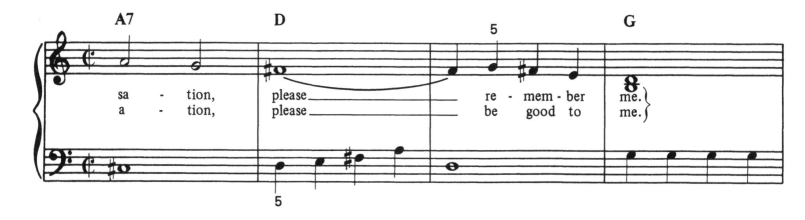

Em7   D6

up, you sil - ly girl;____ Look what you've done.__
out you sil - ly girl;____ See what you've done.__

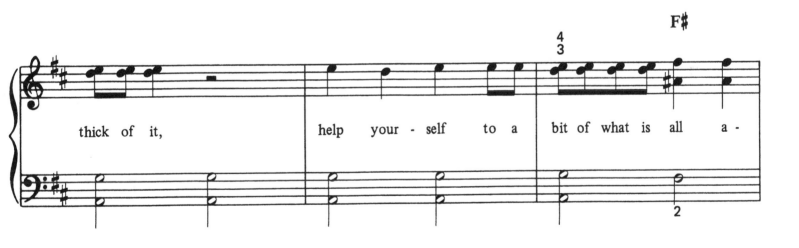

A11

When____ you find____ your - self in the

F#

thick of it, help your - self to a bit of what is all a -

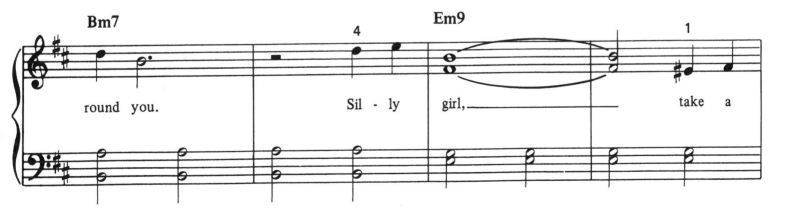

Bm7   Em9

round you. Sil - ly girl,____ take a

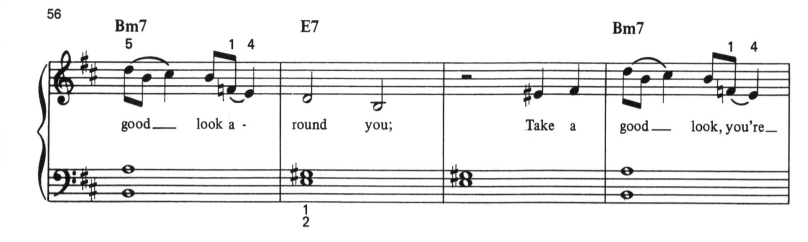

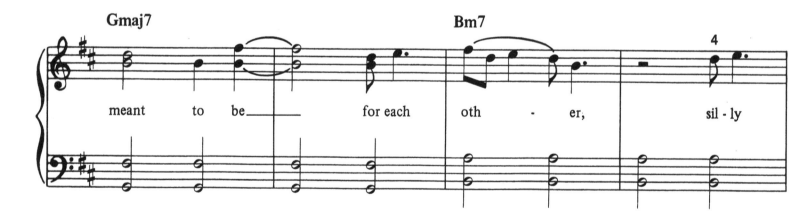

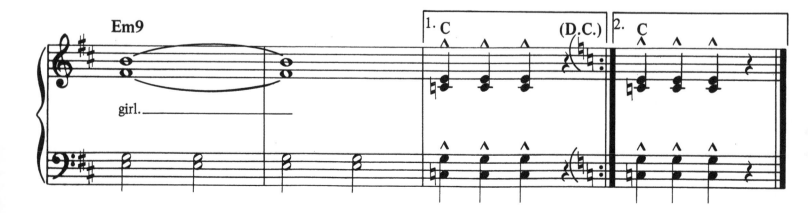

MICHELLE

Words and Music by JOHN LENNON
and PAUL McCARTNEY

Gentle Ballad (but not too slow)

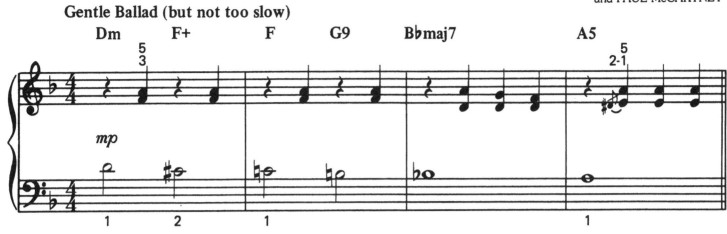

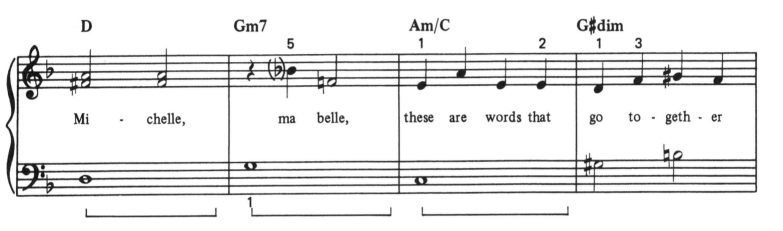

Mi - chelle, ma belle, these are words that go to - geth - er

well, my Mi - chelle.

Mi - chelle,
Mi - chelle,
I love you......

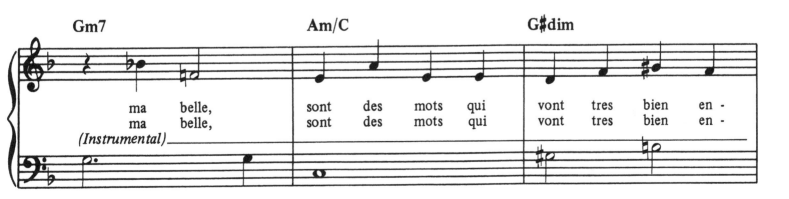

ma belle,
ma belle,
(Instrumental)

sont des mots qui
sont des mots qui

vont tres bien en -
vont tres bien en -

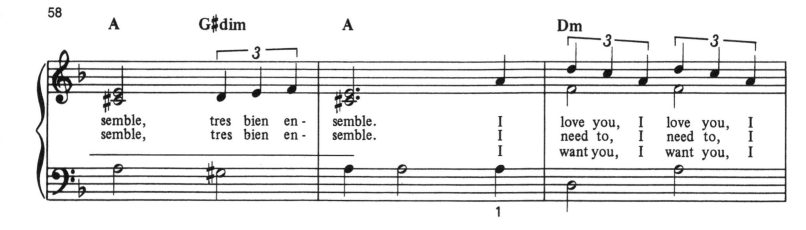

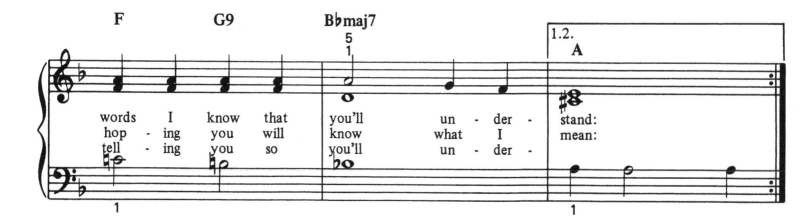

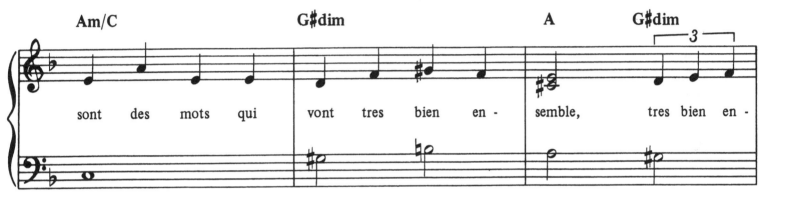

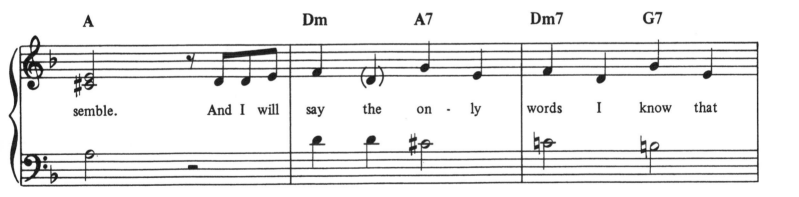

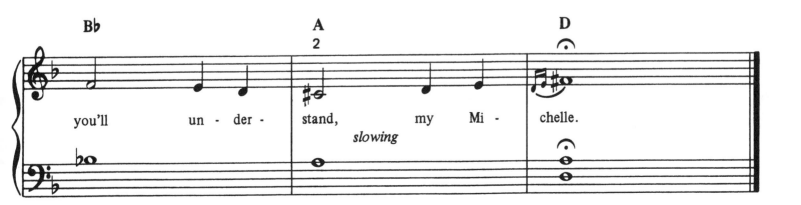

NOWHERE MAN

Words and Music by JOHN LENNON
and PAUL McCARTNEY

Moderate Rock Ballad

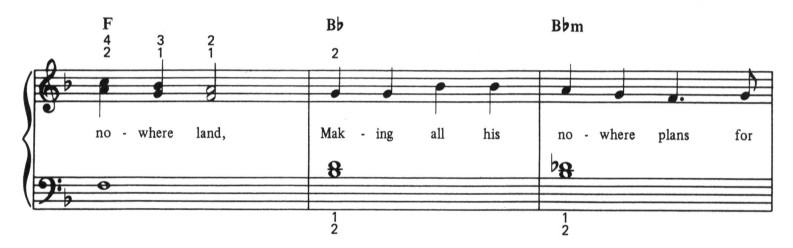

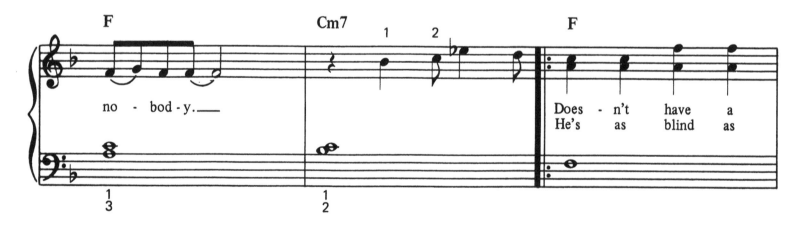

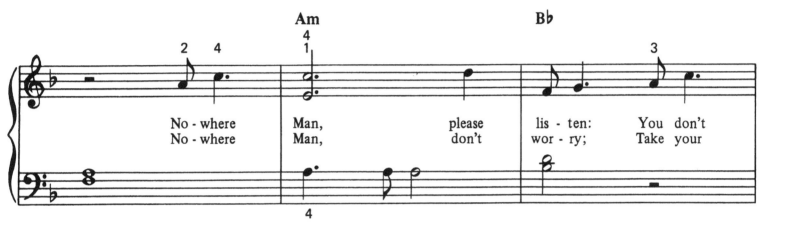

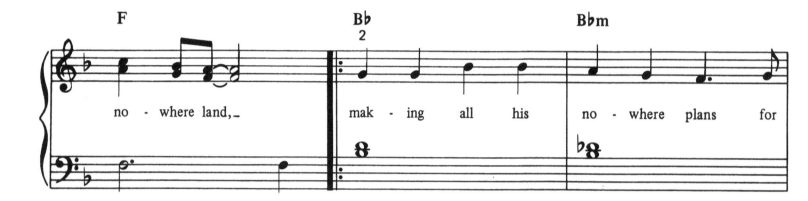

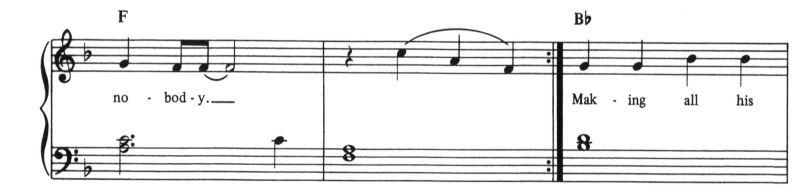

OB-LA-DI, OB-LA-DA

Words and Music by JOHN LENNON
and PAUL McCARTNEY

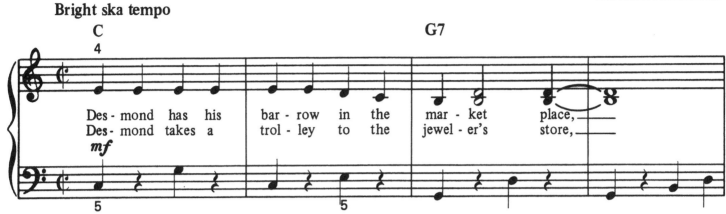

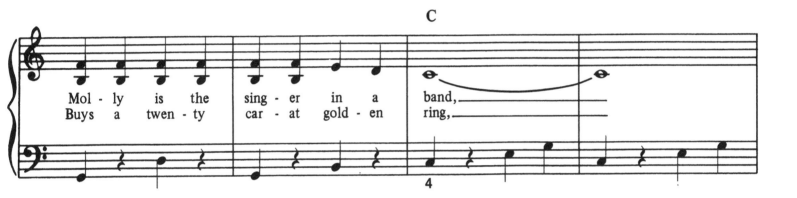

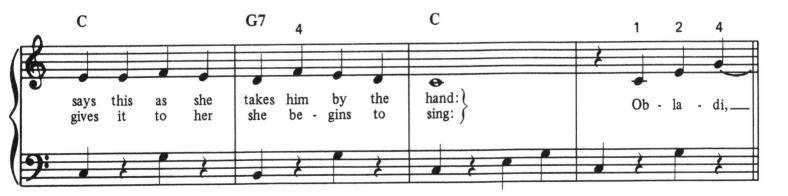

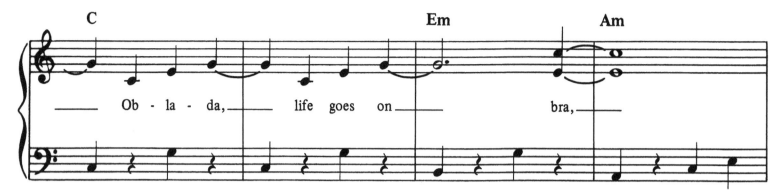

C   Em   Am

Ob - la - da, ____ life goes on ____ bra, ____

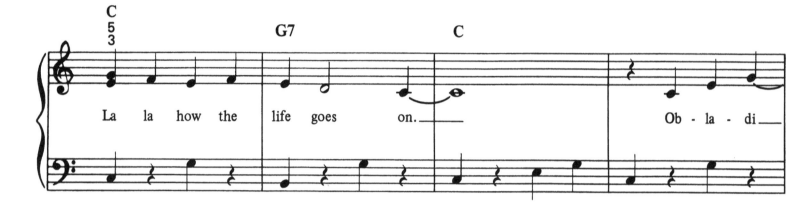

C   5   G7   C
   3

La la how the life goes on. ____ Ob - la - di ____

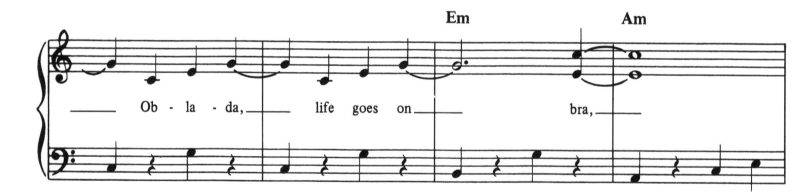

Em   Am

____ Ob - la - da, ____ life goes on ____ bra, ____

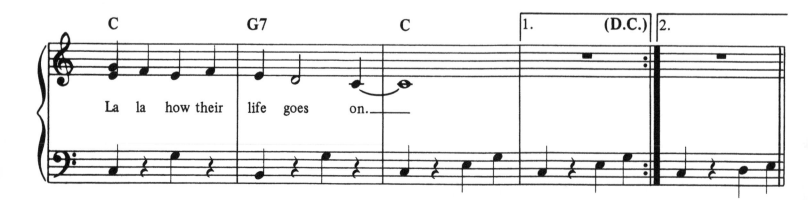

C   G7   C   1.   (D.C.)   2.

La la how their life goes on. ____

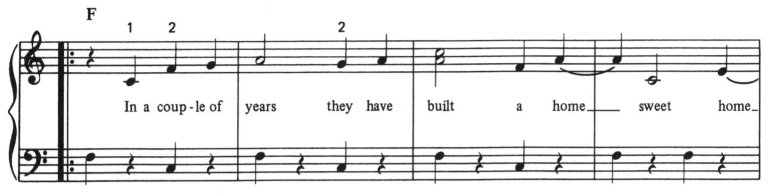

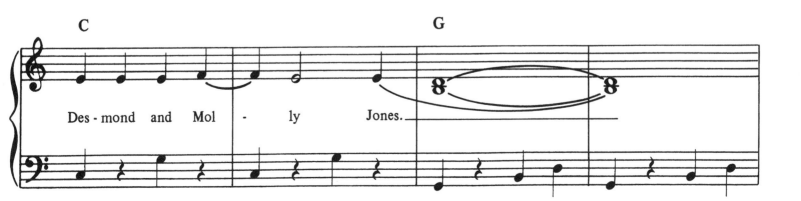

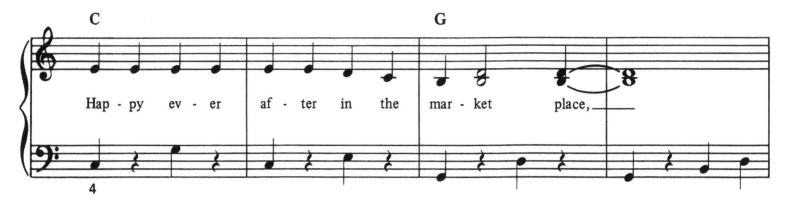

C   **G**

Hap - py ev - er af - ter in the mar - ket place, ___

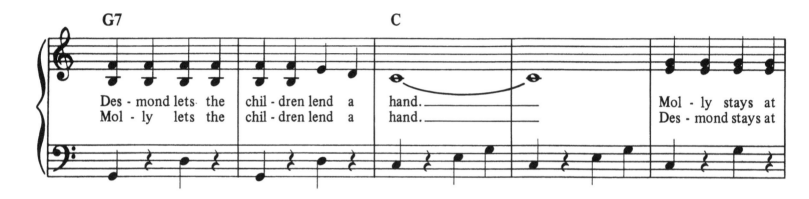

G7   **C**

Des - mond lets the chil - dren lend a hand. ___ Mol - ly stays at
Mol - ly lets the chil - dren lend a hand. ___ Des - mond stays at

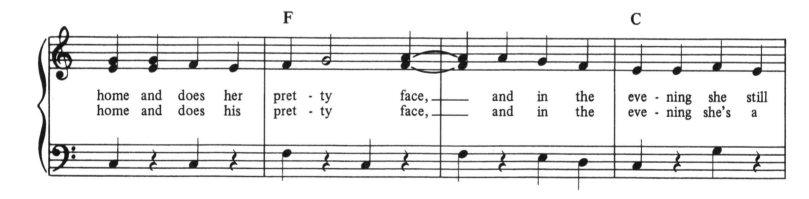

         F   **C**

home and does her pret - ty face, ___ and in the eve - ning she still
home and does his pret - ty face, ___ and in the eve - ning she's a

G7   **C**

sings it with the band: Ob - la - di, ___ ob - la - da, ___ life goes on.
sing - er with the band:

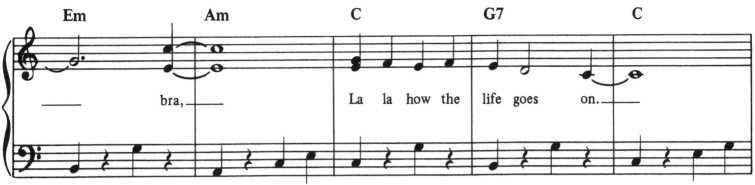

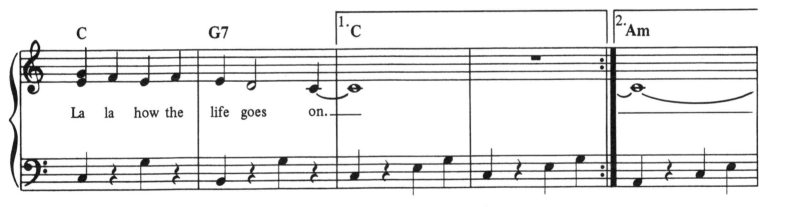

REVOLUTION

Words and Music by JOHN LENNON
and PAUL McCARTNEY

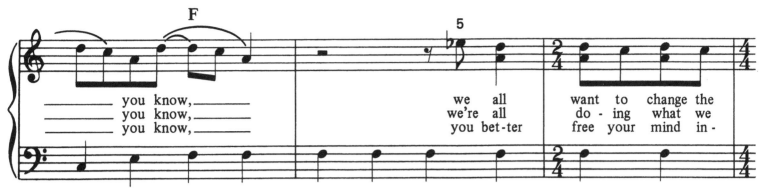

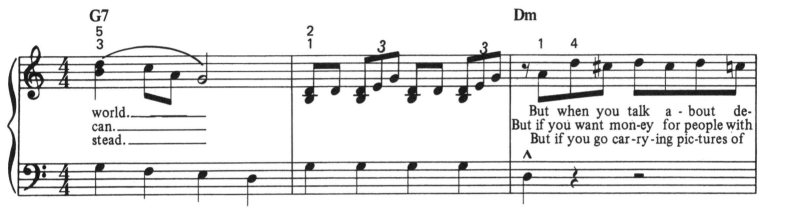

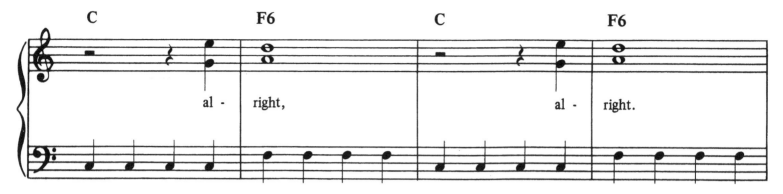

ROCKY RACCOON

Words and Music by JOHN LENNON
and PAUL McCARTNEY

Moderate two-beat style

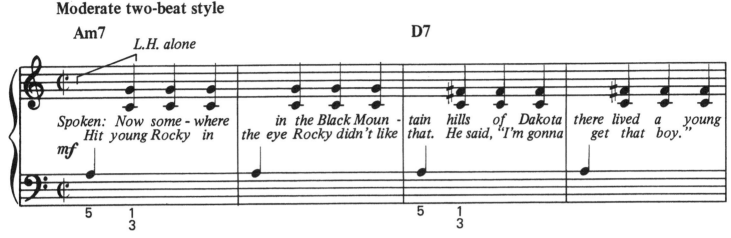

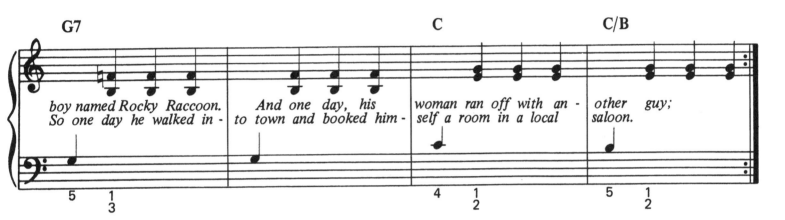

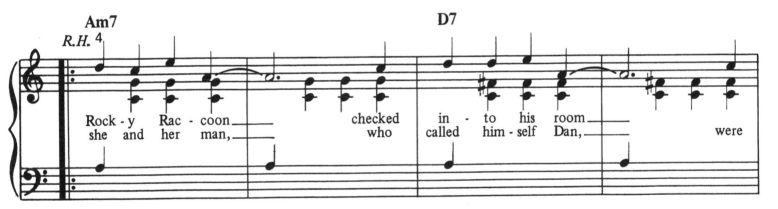

Rock - y had come, _____ e - and quipped with a gun, _____ to
Rock - y burst in, _____ grin - ning a grin, _____ he said,

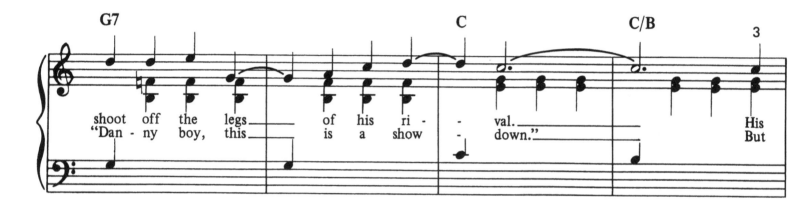

shoot off the legs _____ of his ri - val. His
"Dan - ny boy, this _____ is a show - down." But

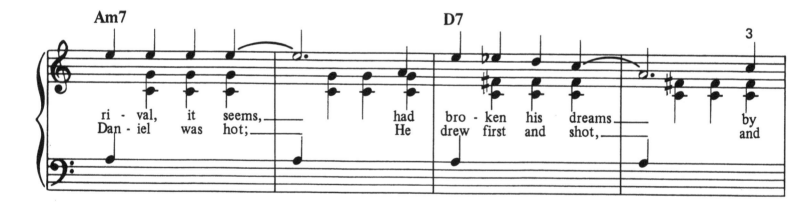

ri - val, it seems, _____ had bro - ken his dreams _____ by
Dan - iel was hot; _____ He drew first and shot, _____ and

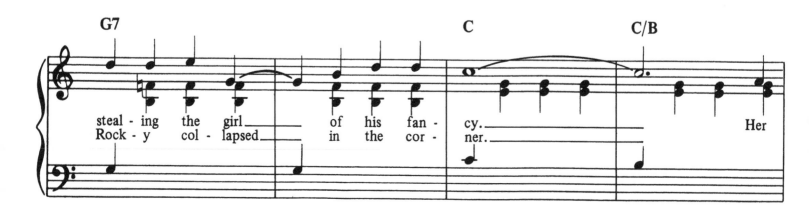

steal - ing the girl _____ of his fan - cy. _____ Her
Rock - y col - lapsed _____ in the cor - ner. _____ Her

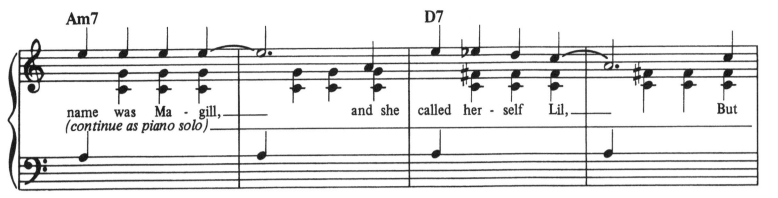

name was Ma - gill, _____ and she called her - self Lil, _____ But
(continue as piano solo) _____

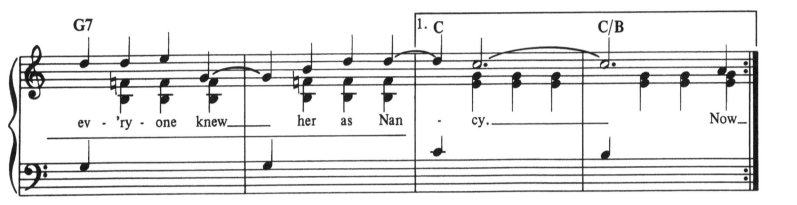

ev - 'ry - one knew____ her as Nan - cy. _____ Now____

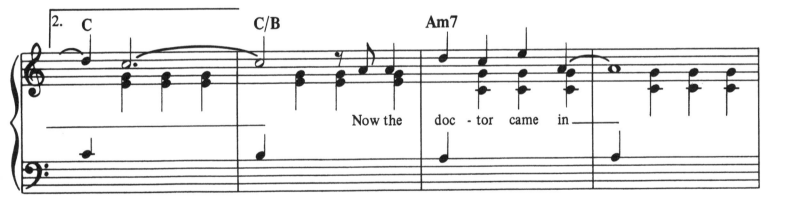

Now the doc - tor came in ____

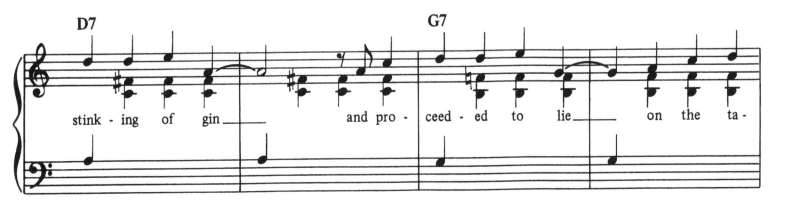

stink - ing of gin _____ and pro - ceed - ed to lie____ on the ta -

ble. He said, "Rock-y, you met ___ your match."

And Rock-y said, "Doc, it's on-ly a scratch, and I'll be

bet-ter, I'll be bet-ter, Doc, as soon ___ as I am a - ble." ___

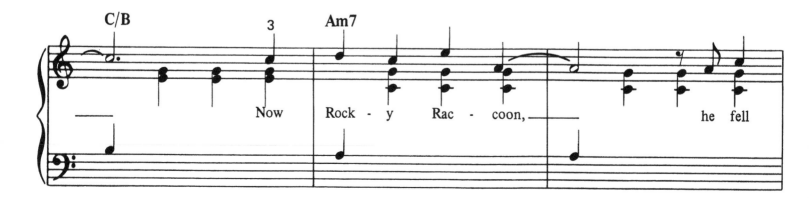

___ Now Rock-y Rac - coon, ___ he fell

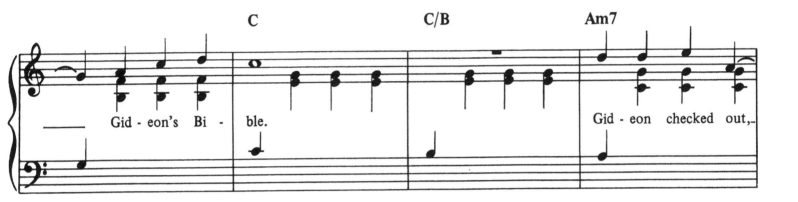

SGT. PEPPER'S LONELY HEARTS CLUB BAND

Words and Music by JOHN LENNON
and PAUL McCARTNEY

Slowly, with a beat

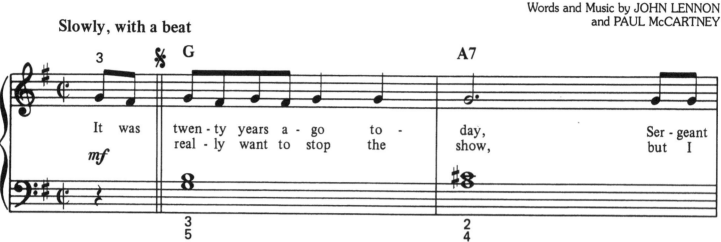

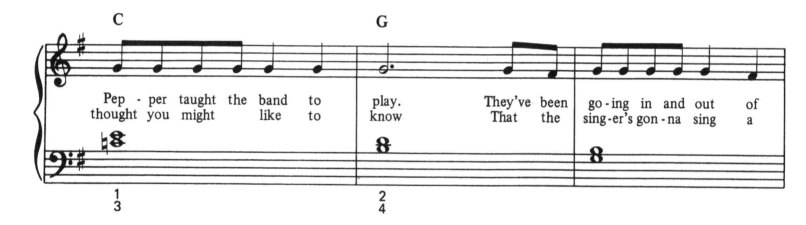

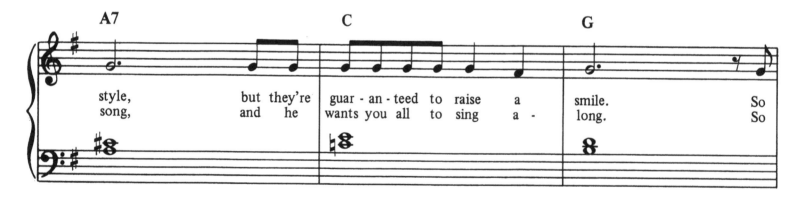

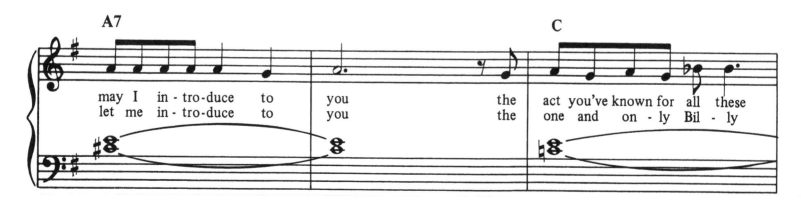

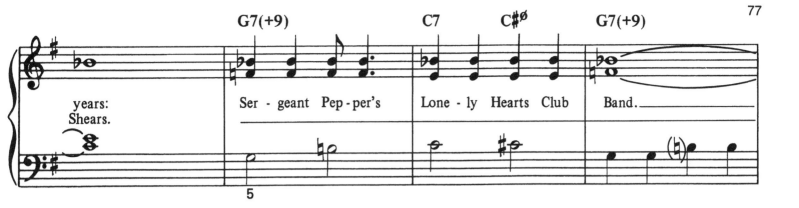

G7(+9)   C7   C#ø   G7(+9)

years: Ser - geant Pep - per's   Lone - ly Hearts Club   Band.
Shears.

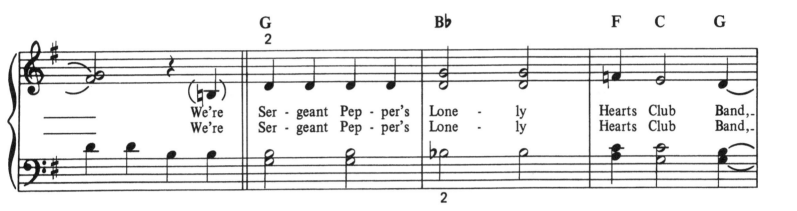

G   Bb   F   C   G

We're   Ser - geant Pep - per's   Lone - ly   Hearts Club   Band,
We're   Ser - geant Pep - per's   Lone - ly   Hearts Club   Band,

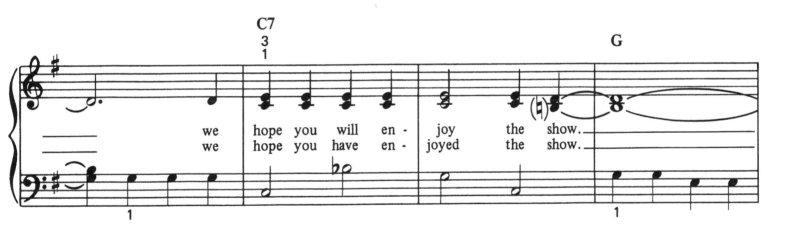

C7   G

we   hope you will en - joy   the show.
we   hope you have en - joyed   the show.

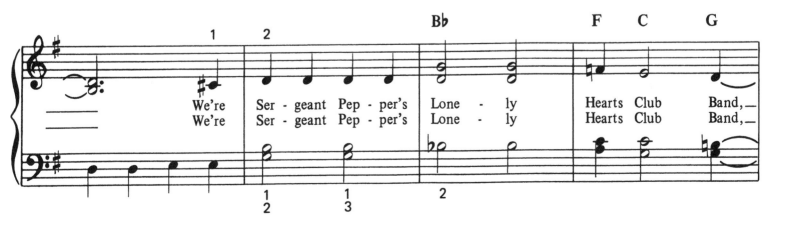

Bb   F   C   G

We're   Ser - geant Pep - per's   Lone - ly   Hearts Club   Band,
We're   Ser - geant Pep - per's   Lone - ly   Hearts Club   Band,

A7 **D7**

sit back and let the eve - ning go.
we're sor - ry but it's time to go.

1

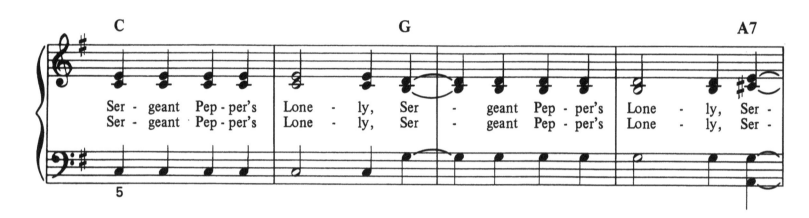

C **G** **A7**

Ser - geant Pep - per's Lone - ly, Ser - geant Pep - per's Lone - ly, Ser -
Ser - geant Pep - per's Lone - ly, Ser - geant Pep - per's Lone - ly, Ser -

5

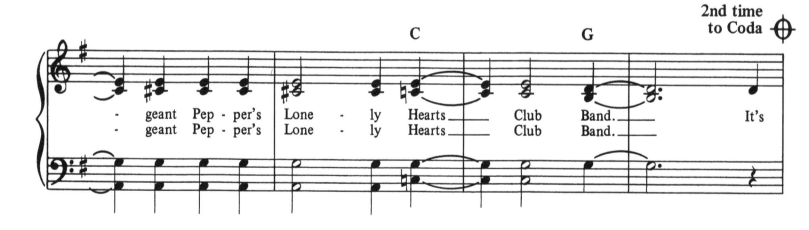

2nd time
to Coda ⊕

C **G**

- geant Pep - per's Lone - ly Hearts Club Band. It's
- geant Pep - per's Lone - ly Hearts Club Band.

C7 **F7**
5 4
1 3

won - der - ful to be here, it's cer - tain - ly a thrill; You're

1

C7

such a love - ly | au - di - ence, we'd | like to take you | home with us, we'd

D.S. al Coda

love to take you | home. I don't

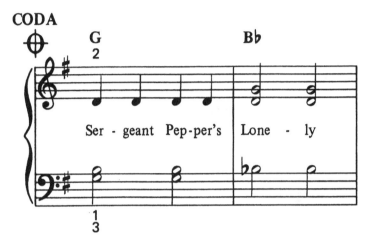

CODA

G Ser - geant Pep - per's Lone - ly

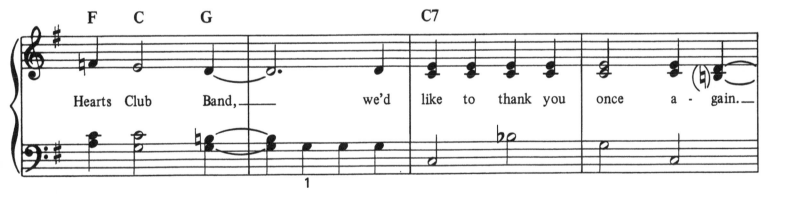

F C G **C7**

Hearts Club Band, _____ we'd like to thank you once a - gain. _____

G **Bb**

Ser - geant Pep - per's one and on - ly

Lone - ly Hearts Club Band, It's get - ting ver - y near the end.___

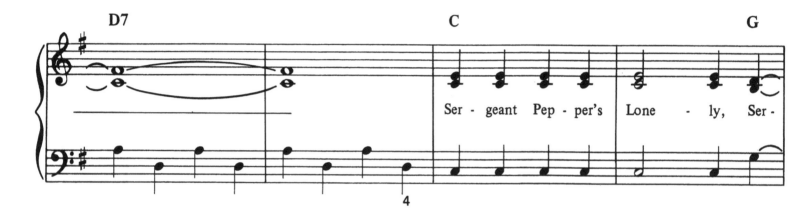

Ser - geant Pep - per's Lone - ly, Ser -

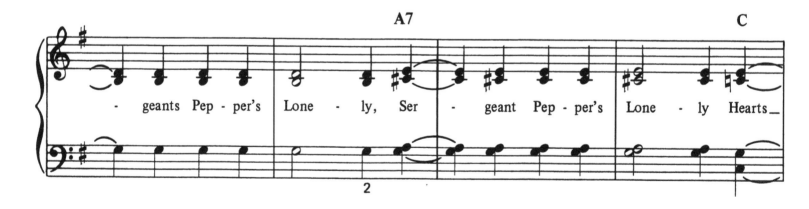

- geants Pep - per's Lone - ly, Ser - geant Pep - per's Lone - ly Hearts___

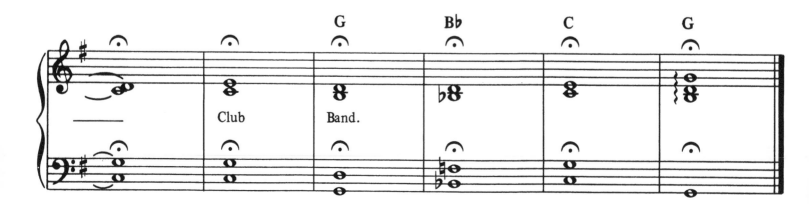

Club Band.

STRAWBERRY FIELDS FOREVER

Words and Music by JOHN LENNON
and PAUL McCARTNEY

Slowly, but not dragging

Let me take you down 'cause I'm go-in' to Straw-ber-ry

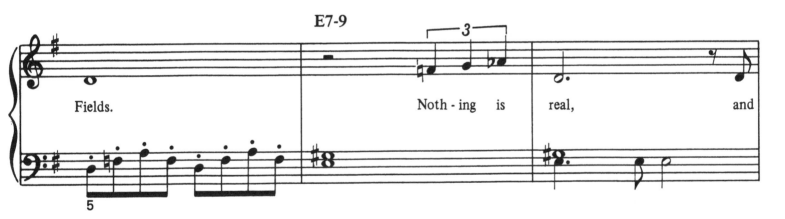

Fields. Noth-ing is real, and

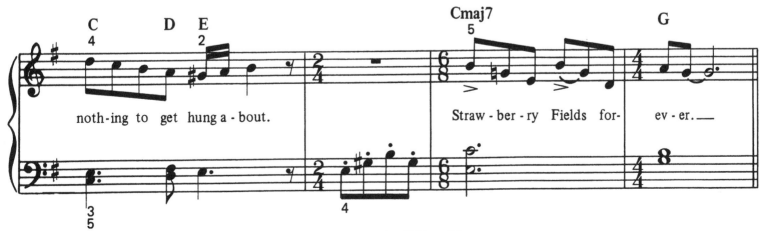

noth-ing to get hung a-bout. Straw-ber-ry Fields for-ev-er.

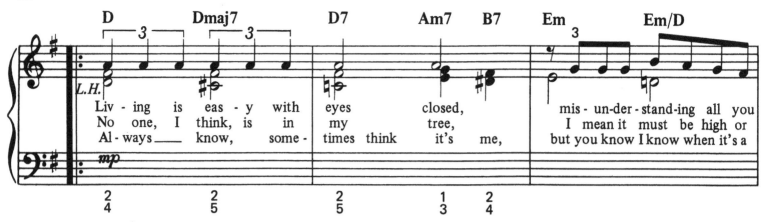

Liv - ing is eas - y with eyes closed, mis - un - der - stand - ing all you
No one, I think, is in my tree, I mean it must be high or
Al - ways __ know, some - times think it's me, but you know I know when it's a

see. It's get - ting hard to be some -
low. That is, you know you can't tune
dream. I think a "no" will be a

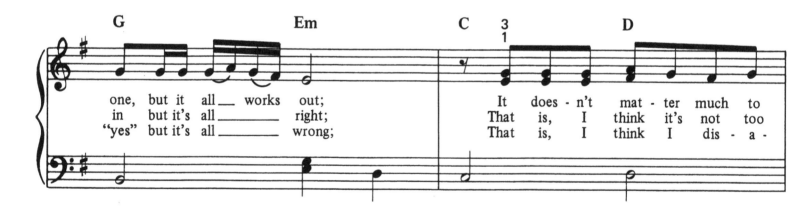

one, but it all __ works out; It does - n't mat - ter much to
in but it's all __ right; That is, I think it's not too
"yes" but it's all __ wrong; That is, I think I dis - a -

me. __
bad. __   Let me take you   down 'cause I'm go - in'
gree. __

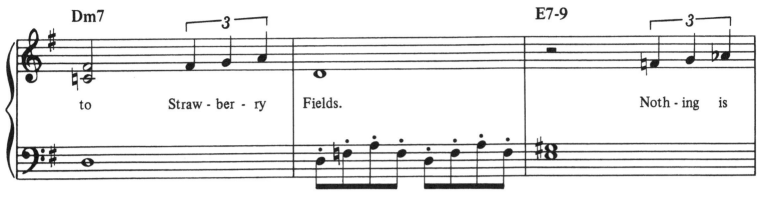

to Straw - ber - ry Fields. Noth - ing is

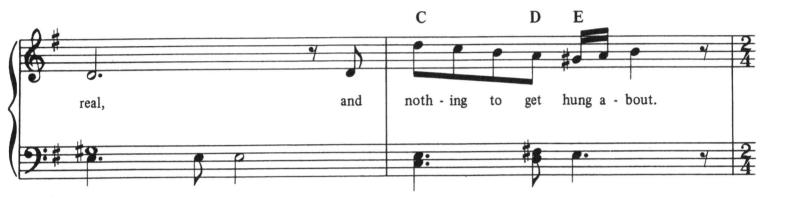

real, and noth - ing to get hung a - bout.

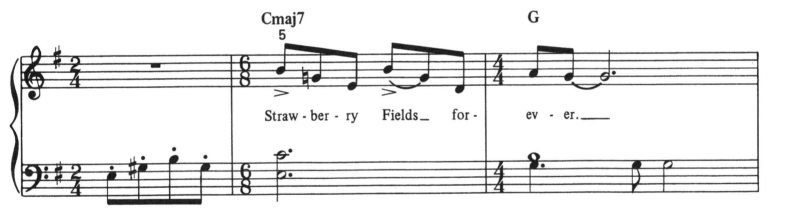

Straw - ber - ry Fields_ for - ev - er.___

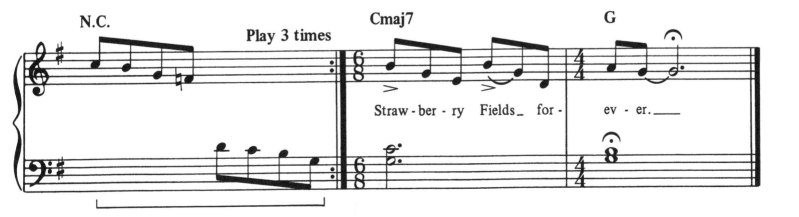

Straw - ber - ry Fields_ for - ev - er.___

TWIST AND SHOUT

Words and Music by BERT RUSSELL
and PHIL MEDLEY

Moderate Rock and Roll beat

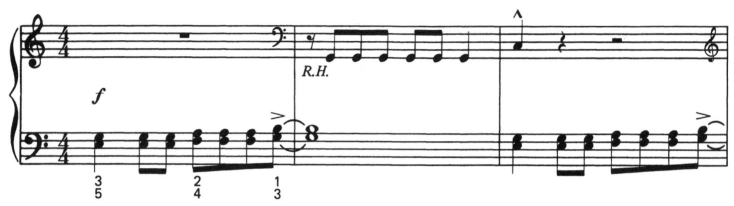

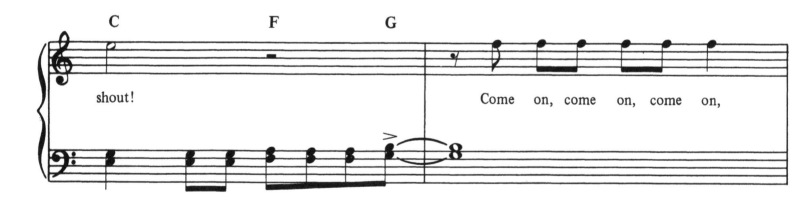

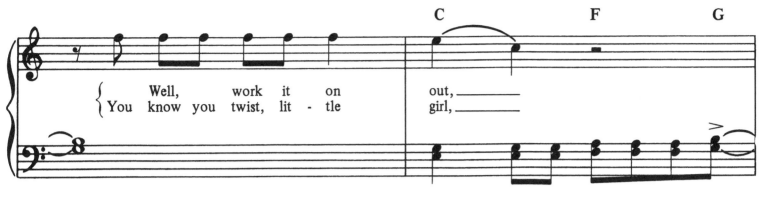

C   F   G

Well,   work it on   out, _____
You know you twist, lit - tle   girl, _____

C   F   G

You know you look so   good; ___   You know you got ___ me ___
You know you twist so   fine ___   Come on and twist a lit - tle

C   F   G   C   F   G

go - in' now,   Just like I knew you   would.
clos - er now,   And let me know that you're   mine.

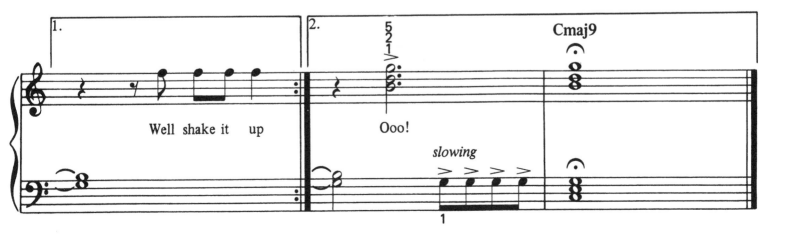

1.
Well shake it up

2.
Cmaj9
Ooo!
slowing

1

TWO OF US

Words and Music by JOHN LENNON
and PAUL McCARTNEY

Brightly, in 2 (♩ = 1 beat)

Two of us, rid - ing no - where, spend - ing some -
Two of us, send - ing post - cards, writ - ing let -
Two of us, wear - ing rain - coats, stand - ing so -

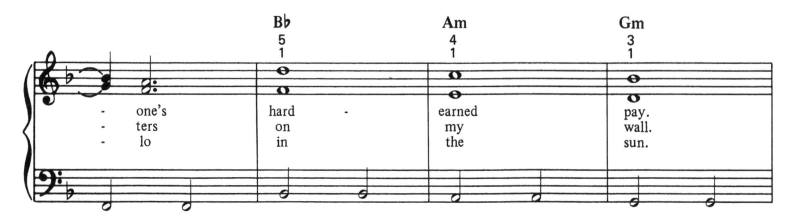

- one's hard - earned pay.
- ters on my wall.
- lo in the sun.

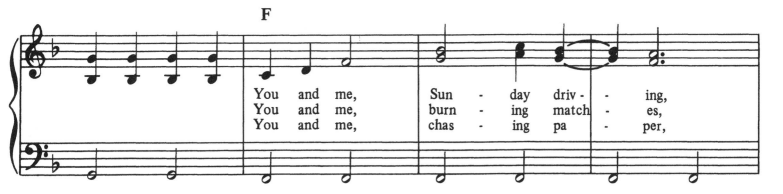

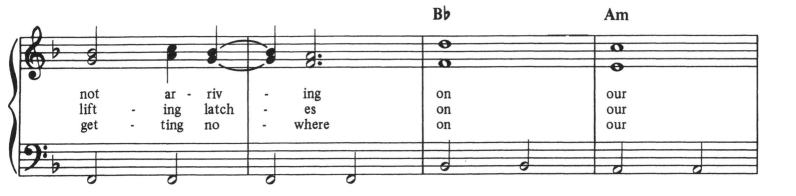

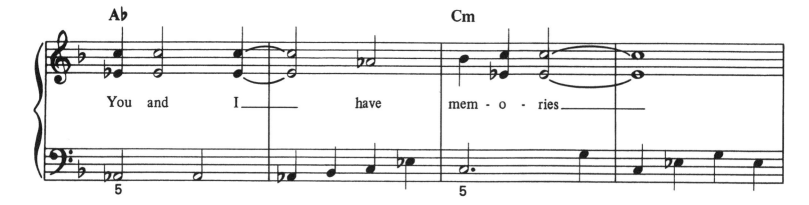

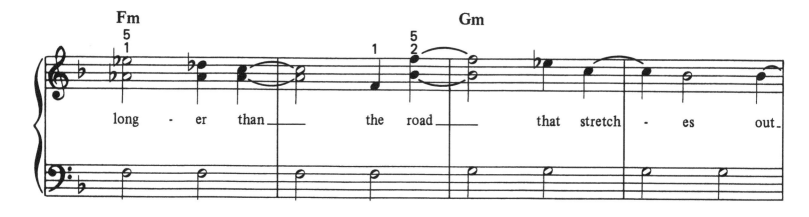

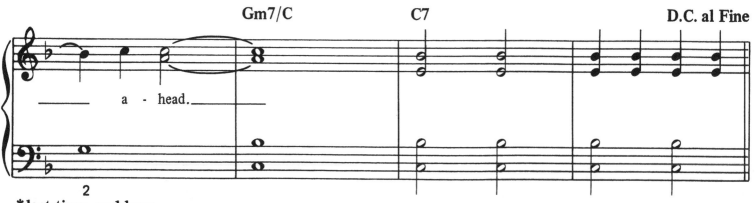

*last time, end here.

YOU WON'T SEE ME

Words and Music by JOHN LENNON
and PAUL McCARTNEY

Moderate Rock

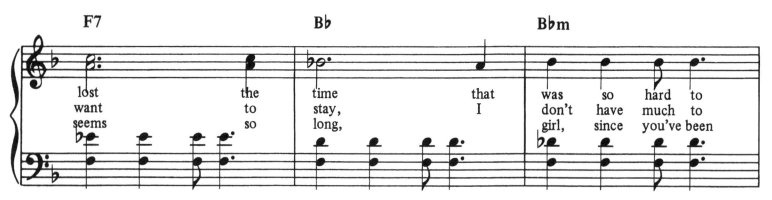

F7   Bb   Bbm

lost   the   time   that   was   so   hard   to
want   to   stay,   I   don't   have   much   to
seems   so   long,   girl,   since   you've been

F   G7

find,   And I will   lose   my   mind   if
say,   But I can   turn   a -   way   and
gone,   And I just   can't   go   on   if

Last time to Coda ⊕

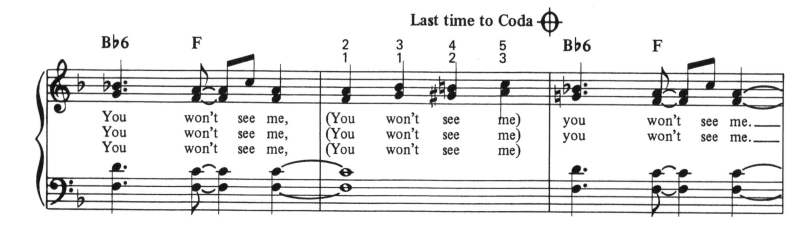

Bb6   F   2 3 4 5   Bb6   F
            1 1 2 3

You   won't see me,   (You won't see me)   you   won't see me.___
You   won't see me,   (You won't see me)   you   won't see me.___
You   won't see me,   (You won't see me)   you   won't see me.

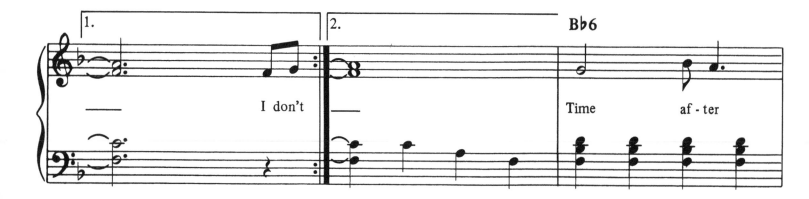

1.   2.   Bb6

___   I don't   ___   Time   af - ter

Bbm6 ... **F**

time you re- | fuse to e - ven lis - ten;

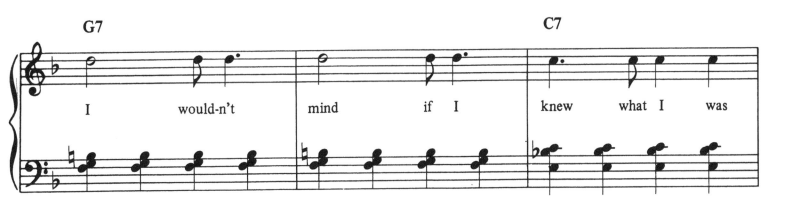

G7 ... **C7**

I would-n't | mind if I | knew what I was

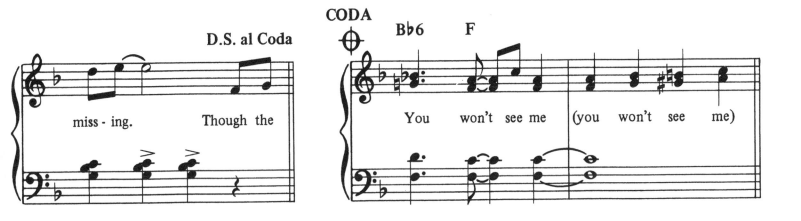

D.S. al Coda | **CODA** **Bb6** **F**

miss - ing. Though the | You won't see me | (you won't see me)

F ... **G7** ... **Bb** ... **F** Repeat and Fade

La la la, | la la la, | la la la, | la la la,

WITH A LITTLE HELP FROM MY FRIENDS

Words and Music by JOHN LENNON
and PAUL McCARTNEY

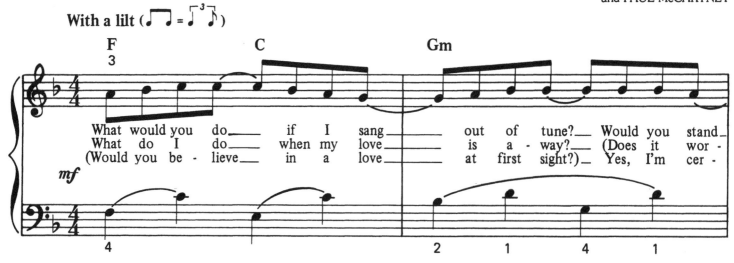

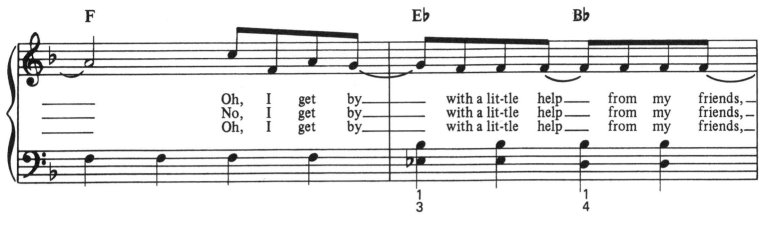

Oh, I get by___ with a lit-tle help___ from my friends,___
No, I get by___ with a lit-tle help___ from my friends,__
Oh, I get by___ with a lit-tle help___ from my friends,___

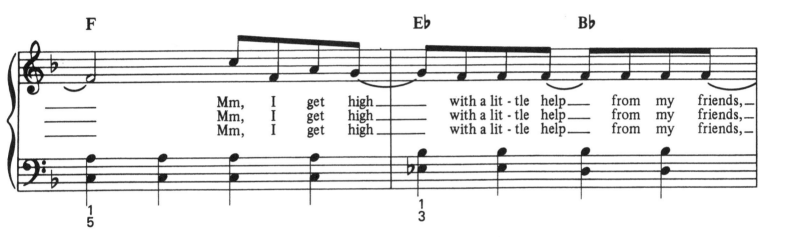

Mm, I get high___ with a lit-tle help___ from my friends,___
Mm, I get high___ with a lit-tle help___ from my friends,__
Mm, I get high___ with a lit-tle help___ from my friends,___

Mm, I'm gon-na try with a lit-tle help___ from my friends.___
Mm, I'm gon-na try with a lit-tle help___ from my friends.___
Mm, I'm gon-na try with a lit-tle help___ from my friends.___

(Do you
(Do you

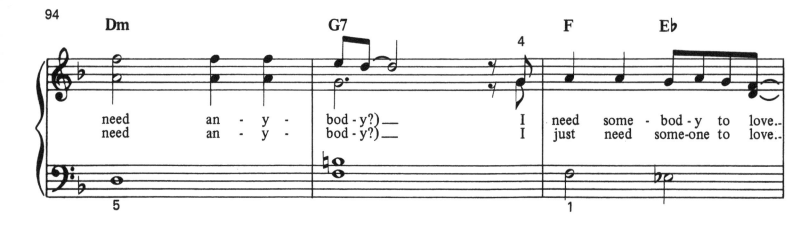

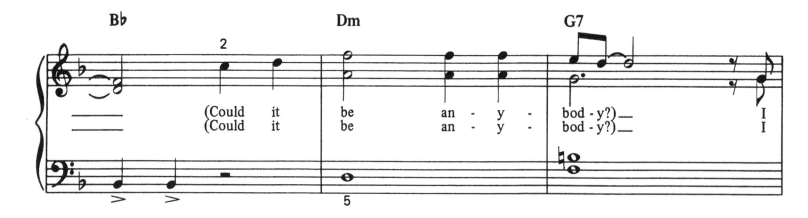

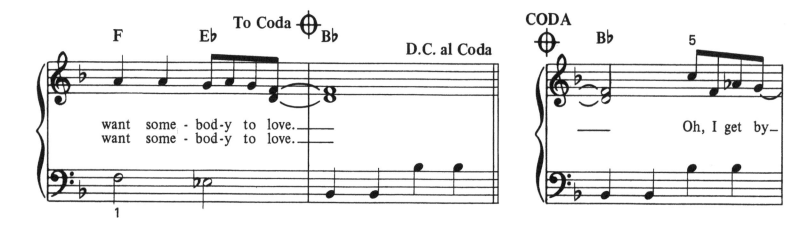

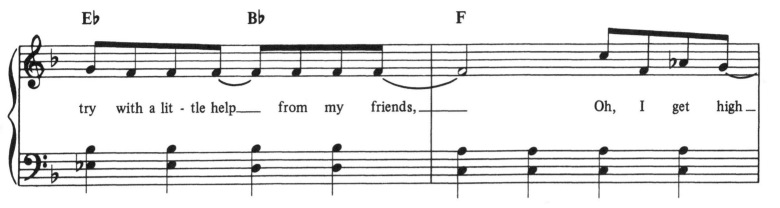

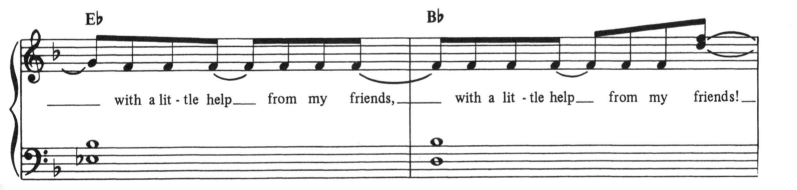